Think Right,
LIVE WELL

Think Right, LIVE WELL

DAILY REFLECTIONS

with Archbishop Fulton J. Sheen

EDITED BY BERT GHEZZI

Our Sunday Visitor

www.osv.com
Our Sunday Visitor Publishing Division
Our Sunday Visitor, Inc.
Huntington, Indiana 46750

Introduction, prayers, and arrangement of texts: Copyright © 2017 by Our Sunday Visitor Publishing Division. Published 2017.

22 21 20 19 18 17   1 2 3 4 5 6 7 8 9

Our Sunday Visitor Publishing Division, Our Sunday Visitor, Inc., 200 Noll Plaza, Huntington, IN 46750; 1-800-348-2440

ISBN: 978-1-61278-872-2 (Inventory No. T1666)
eISBN: 978-1-61278-874-6
LCCN: 2017944350

Cover design: Amanda Falk
Cover art: background: Shutterstock; photo: Our Sunday Visitor file photo
Interior design: Sherri L. Hoffman
Interior art: Photo on page 5 courtesy of Bert Ghezzi

PRINTED IN THE UNITED STATES OF AMERICA

About the Editor

BERT GHEZZI is a popular author and speaker. He has written twenty books, including *Voices of the Saints, Mystics and Miracles*, and most recently, *Prayers to the Holy Spirit* and *The Power of Daily Mass*. Hundreds of Bert's articles have appeared in the Catholic and religious press.

Bert has been involved in all levels of religious education for more than forty years. He has served as a leader and teacher in several Catholic renewal movements. Numerous educational and renewal conferences throughout the United States and Canada have featured Bert as a speaker. He appears frequently as a guest on EWTN programs. EWTN also features his series *Signs of Our Times*. Bert is often interviewed on Catholic radio networks. His two-minute spots on saints play regularly on EWTN radio.

After receiving his Ph.D. from the University of Notre Dame, Bert served for seven years as a professor at Grand Valley State University, Allendale, Michigan. From 1975 to 2016, he served as a senior editor for five publishing companies.

Bert has seven adult children and sixteen grandchildren. He is an active member of St. Mary Magdalen Catholic Church and lives near the church in Altamonte Springs, Florida. His website is www .bertghezzi.com.

Contents

Introduction

In the 1950s, Fulton J. Sheen emerged as television's very first popular religious communicator. As a kid, I enjoyed watching him on Tuesday nights at eight o'clock. The DuMont Television Network launched his program, *Life Is Worth Living*, in 1951, with modest expectations, as the network had put him up against both Milton Berle and Frank Sinatra. But his smart formula of down-home humor, clear exposition, and no proselytization made him an immediate success.

In his first year—out of a field that included Lucille Ball, Arthur Godfrey, Jimmy Durante, and Edward R. Murrow—Sheen (he became an archbishop in 1969) won the Emmy for Most Outstanding Television Personality. When he accepted the award, he said, "I feel it's time I paid tribute to my writers—Matthew, Mark, Luke, and John." By 1954, his ratings competed favorably with those of "Mr. Television" himself, Milton Berle. Berle, known as "Uncle Miltie," became Bishop Sheen's friend. Berle also nicknamed him "Uncle Fultie," and once quipped that "he used old material too." In 1956, *Life Is Worth Living* had moved to ABC television, was being broadcast on 187 stations, and drew as many as 30 million viewers every week.

Without a doubt, Archbishop Sheen stands as the preeminent Catholic media evangelist of the twentieth century. In the 1930s and 1940s, millions listened to his weekly radio teachings on *The Catholic Hour.* Over six decades, from the time of his ordination to the priesthood in 1919, Sheen gave thousands of talks to groups in the United States and throughout the world. During this time, he published more than sixty best-selling books, mostly popular presentations of practical teaching on growing in faith. From 1925 to 1950, he taught philosophy to hundreds of students as a professor at The Catholic University of America. And in 1950, Pope Pius XII appointed Sheen as the national director of the American branch of the Society for the Propagation of the Faith. For three decades, he used this platform to evangelize thousands and raised millions of dollars to serve the needs of the poor and marginalized throughout the world.

Over the years in his broadcasts, talks, and books, Fulton Sheen honed his skill at turning an apt phrase that would capture attention. He expressed his famous sense of humor, for example, in quips such as "Hearing nuns' confessions is like being stoned to death with popcorn" and "An atheist is a man who has no invisible means of support." But as you will see in this book, he also had a knack for creating profound expressions that touched people's hearts.

Archbishop Sheen was convinced that if people shaped their minds with the truth, they would live well, they would please God, and they would become saints. This book presents daily quotes of the main themes he advocated. Among them are:

- The centrality of the cross in God's plan and our accepting it as the pattern for our lives.

- The marvelous exchange Jesus made by lowering himself to become a man so that he could elevate us to living a share in his divine life.

- The power unleashed in our lives by doing everything for love of God and neighbor.

- The service of others, especially the poor, by personal care and generous giving.

Archbishop Sheen himself lived by these truths. All his life he patiently bore the cross of criticism, opposition, and even ridicule. Every day, for more than six decades, he spent an hour in adoration of the Blessed Sacrament. Stories of his love, personal care, and generosity abound. He never hung on to cash, giving money freely to anyone who asked and donating all of his book royalties to charity. He often gave his coats or sweaters to needy persons he encountered on the street. And much, much more.

My favorite Sheen story typifies his compassion. Once he welcomed into his life a man so disfigured by Hansen's disease that the man was rejected by family and could not find work. The man met Sheen at St. Patrick's Cathedral in New York, saying, "I have no friends." Sheen replied, "Well, you have one now." He got the man set up in an apartment, found him a job, and invited him to his table once a week, personally cutting up his food. Many years later, when Sheen was installed as the bishop of Rochester, he seated his friend as an honored guest in the sanctuary.

I hope you hear Archbishop Sheen's voice in this book, assuring you that your life is worth living. His message to you is that if you think right, you will live well.

BERT GHEZZI

Eternal Happiness

My wish for you is that you will have a Happy New Year—but by a new year I do not mean in the sense of another . . . there is no happiness in adding year to year and growing older. By a new year I mean new in the sense of regenerated, rejuvenated, new-born, for there is happiness in having life before you—especially the Eternal Life of God.

The Prodigal World, 9

⌒

Thank you, Lord, for the gift of Eternal Life, the source of my happiness.

Beliefs Direct Behavior

It does make a tremendous difference what we believe, for we act on our beliefs. If our beliefs are right, our deeds will be right.

Philosophies at War, 25

~

Lord, fill my mind and heart with wisdom so that all I do will be pleasing to you.

Thirsting for God

To be worthy of the name Christian ... means that we, too, must thirst for the spread of the Divine Love; if we do not thirst, then we shall never be invited to sit down at the banquet of Life.

The Rainbow of Sorrow, 70

Lord, let the Holy Spirit flow like a river from my heart. May he inspire and strengthen me to spread your love to those who long for you.

True Humility

Humility is truth. A humble man neither praises nor belittles himself. Underestimation can be as false as overestimation.... The humble man makes room for progress; the proud man believes he is already there.

On Being Human, 66

~

O Holy Spirit, give me always a true perspective on myself and my gifts.

Never Before . . .

Never before in the history of the world was there so much knowledge; and never before so little coming to the knowledge of the Truth. Never before so much straining for life; never before so many unhappy lives. Never before so much science; never before was it used so for the destruction of human life.

Seven Pillars of Peace, 181–182

Lord Jesus, may I come to know you more fully, you who are the Way, the Truth, and the Life.

God with Us

No man can love anything unless he can get his arms around it, and the cosmos is too big and too bulky. But once God became a Babe and was wrapped in swaddling clothes and laid in a manger, men could say, "This is Emmanuel, this is God with us."

Life of Christ, 31

How wonderful it is, Lord Jesus, that you came to be with me.

A Human Contradiction

Original sin alone can explain the almost contradictory character of human nature which makes a man aspire to higher things and at the same time succumb to the baser. The only reason we seek the nobler things of God is that we once possessed them; we seek because once we found.

The Divine Romance, 40

Lord, I turn the eyes of my heart to heavenly things so that I can conduct myself well on earth.

Glimpses of God

Though God freely wills to reveal Himself to creatures He does it only progressively. He does not immediately draw the veil that hides His august majesty. He merely gives His creatures little glimpses and reserves the full vision for heaven.... And each new revelation has made Him better known and better loved.

The Life of All Living, 51

O Lord, I want to come to know you more and more.

A Leader Worth Following

If Jesus is what He claimed to be, a Savior, a Redeemer, then we have a virile Christ and a leader worth following in these terrible times; One Who will step into the breach of death, crushing sin, gloom and despair; a leader to Whom we can make a total sacrifice without losing but gaining freedom, and Whom we can love even unto death.

Life of Christ, 21

Jesus, I give myself to you; be with me when I am troubled.

The World's Greatest Need

The world's greatest need ... is someone who will understand that there is no greater conquest than victory over oneself; someone who will realize that real worth is achieved not so much by activity, as by silence; who will seek first the Kingdom of God and His justice, and put into actual practice the law that it is only by dying to the life of the body that we ever live to the life of the Spirit.

Moods and Truths, 21

I want to be that someone, Lord, that the world needs.
I put a priority on seeking your kingdom and giving
you my life.

Know Yourself

Self-knowledge is not intellectual, but moral. It falls not within the domain of psychology, but theology; it is concerned not with what we think, but with our motives and the hidden springs of life and action.

Love One Another, 80

Holy Spirit, probe my mind and heart and show me the motives that drive my conduct.

The Communion of Saints

Few consolations are greater than the knowledge that we are bound up in a great corporation of prayers and sacrifices. The Communion of Saints is the great discovery of those, who, as adults, find the fullness of faith. They discover that for years there have been dozens, in some cases hundreds, of souls praying especially for them.

Peace of Soul, 211

May the merits and prayers of the saints comfort and strengthen me.

Salt and Light

Away with mediocrity! Lift up your hearts! The world is looking for light. Will you hide yours under bushels? The earth is looking for savor; will you let the salt lose its savor?

The Cross and the Beatitudes, 68

~

I lift up my heart to you, Lord, and I pledge to let my light shine brightly in my world.

The Purpose of Love

Love was meant to be a sign, a symbol, of the Divine. No man is the final goal of any woman, nor is any woman the ultimate purpose of any man. God is the end of both. Each person has the Infinite within him; it is that we are after.

The Power of Love, 26

~

May all my loves, O God, stand in second place to my love for you.

A Finished Life

Real Christians are they who persevere to the end. Our Lord stayed until He had finished.... So we must stay with the Cross until our lives are finished. Christ on the Cross is the Pattern and Model of a finished life.

The Prodigal World, 136

Lord Jesus, looking to your cross, I surrender to all the crosses in my life.

Understanding Mary

The key to understanding Mary is this: We do not start with Mary. We start with Christ, the Son of the Living God! The less we think of Him, the less we think of her; the more we adore His Divinity, the more we venerate her Motherhood.

The World's First Love, 67

I adore you, Lord Jesus, and honor your Mother and mine.

Making Others Happy

Cheerfulness is that quality which enables one to make others happy. It takes origin half in personal goodness, and half in the belief of the personal goodness of others. It is the opposite of the morbid, the morose, the fretful, the grumbling, the somber.

Guide to Contentment, 147

God, fill my heart with joy so that I may bring good cheer to others.

Someone Cares

Because Someone cares, we care; because I am loved in my miserable self, I must love others who certainly are better than I. If Someone took on my burden of guilt, then I must be forgiving to others.

Footprints in a Darkened Forest, 104

As you love and forgive me, may I love and forgive my family, friends, and acquaintances.

Real Progress

Every advance toward racial justice, every move toward the improvement of the actual human condition, every striving of nations to unite in the peaceful settlement of disputes, every picking up of the pieces of the broken world and putting them together is a heightened form of service which is love.

Footprints in a Darkened Forest, 93

Lord, may I serve you in the poor, the marginalized, and all those treated unjustly.

Honoring Mary and the Real Presence

On the day of my Ordination, I made two resolutions:
1. I would offer the Holy Eucharist every Saturday in
honor of the Blessed Mother in order to solicit her protection on my priesthood. . . . 2. I resolved to spend a contin-
uous Holy Hour every day in the presence of Our Lord in
the Blessed Sacrament.

Treasure in Clay, 187

*Lord, I promise to take time daily to worship you and
to honor your Mother, Mary.*

Ladders to the Spiritual

In the broad meaning of the term, everything in the world may be regarded as a sacrament in the sense that every material thing is a means, an instrument, a stepping-stone, a scaffolding, a ladder to the spiritual, the infinite, the eternal.

Religion Without God, 305

May I see you in the wonders of your creation, and may they draw me nearer to you.

Light and Heat

Fire has two qualities: light and heat. Light corresponds to truth for the mind, and heat corresponds to love for the will. The two were always meant to go together, in order that enthusiasm would always match faith and knowledge.

Thinking Life Through, 11

Illumine my mind with your light, O Lord, and set my heart on fire with your love.

Communion Makes Us One

Communion is not only incorporation into the life of Christ and incorporation into His death, but it is also communion with all the other members of the Mystical Body of Christ. When we receive Communion we are being united with every other member of the Church throughout the world. . . . The Eucharist makes the Church one.

Your Life Is Worth Living, 207–208

Lord Jesus, help me to appreciate and experience my union with you and the members of your Body.

The Purpose of the State

The primary end of political and social life is the conservation, the development, and the perfection of the human person as a creature made in the image and likeness of God. Hence the state exists for man, not man for the State.

Philosophies at War, 70

⁓

O God, draw all the leaders of our government nearer to you and guide them in their service.

Love Brings Freedom

God is the very embodiment of love. Love inspires you to be what you were meant to be, a free person in the highest sense of the word. The more you are led by God's love, the more you become yourself and it is all done without ever losing your freedom.

Your Life Is Worth Living, 17

May I grow in your love, Lord, and become the person you want me to be.

Wise Passiveness

In silence, there is humility of spirit or what might be called "wise passiveness." In such the ear is more important than the tongue. God speaks, but not in cyclones—only in zephyrs and gentle breezes. As the scientist learns by sitting passively before nature, so the soul learns wisdom by being responsive to His Will.

Way to Inner Peace, 148

Lord God, I want to live in your presence and listen to what you are saying to me.

Open-Handed Prayer

God has two kinds of gifts—those He gives us whether we pray or not, and those He gives on condition we place ourselves in the area of His love. God may want to give us something but cannot, because our hands are full of tinsel.

Life Is Worth Living (Second Series), 113

⁓

O Holy Spirit, I open myself to receive your love and your gifts.

True Happiness

This is happiness—service, encounter, responsibility, availability to all in need for Love's sake.

Footprints in a Darkened Forest, 104

~

Give me opportunities, Lord Jesus, to express my love in service to others.

A New Humanity

When God took upon Himself the human nature and became Christ through the Virgin Mother, He was the first note in the new melody. It is up to our personal will freely to incorporate ourselves to Him by faith, thus adding another note and creating a new humanity.

Life Is Worth Living (First and Second Series), 130

I am delighted, Jesus, that you have united me to yourself in the Church, the community of the new humanity.

Working for Heaven

A heaven of Divine Truth, Righteousness, and Justice would be a hell to those who never studiously cultivated those virtues here below. Heaven is only for those who work for heaven.

Victory Over Vice, 76

~

O God, grant me the graces I need to grow in faith, hope, love, and all the virtues that lead to heaven.

Super-Humanity

Man's true end lies not in mere humanity, but in a kind of super-humanity where he is governed by new laws, vivified by a new soul, and thrilled with new joys. His nature after the manner of the Incarnation has been "assumed" by a higher nature and elevated unto a higher life.

The Mystical Body of Christ, 238

⁓

Lord, show me how to experience and enjoy the super-natural life I enjoy as your disciple.

Yes or No

Life is a tremendous drama in which one may say "Aye" or "Nay" to his eternal destiny. To admit light to the eye, music to the ear and food to the stomach is to perfect each of these organs; so too, to admit Truth to the mind and Power to the will is to make us more than a creature, namely, a partaker in the Divine Nature.

Go to Heaven, viii

~

Lord, I say an unqualified "yes" to all that you intend for me and to all that you have for me.

Philosophies of Life

There are two philosophies of life. One is the pagan philosophy: First the feast, then the headache. The other is the Christian philosophy of life: First the fast, then the feast. Our law is first Good Friday, then Easter Sunday. First the cross, then the empty tomb.

St. Thérèse: A Treasured Love Story, 62

O Resurrected Lord, help me daily to carry my cross with grace and hope.

Conversing with Christ

The purpose of the Holy Hour is to encourage deep personal encounter with Christ. The holy and glorious God is constantly inviting us to come to Him, to hold converse with Him, to ask for such things as we need and to experience what a blessing there is in fellowship with Him.

Treasure in Clay, 190

I adore you, Lord Jesus, and I come into your presence to have a conversation with you.

The Assurance of God's Mercy

Oh, what greater assurance is there in all the world of the mercy of God? Lost sheep, prodigal sons, broken Magdalens, penitent Peters, forgiven thieves! Such is the rosary of Divine forgiveness.

The Seven Last Words, 17

O Lord, I line up with all these penitents to ask your forgiveness for my sins.

Thinking Right About Life

The choice before our generation is between an organic spiritual unity and an organized technical unity, or between a philosophy of life which says that man is a potential child of God and a philosophy of life which says that there is no God but Caesar.

The Cross and the Crisis, viii

~

I will live my life according to your ways, O Lord, as a child in your divine family.

Shaping Children for God

Every child is a potential nobleman for the Kingdom of God. Parents are to take that living stone from the quarry of humanity, cut and chisel it by loving discipline, sacrifice, mold it on the pattern of the Christ-Truth until it becomes a fit stone for the Temple of God, whose architect is Love.

Philosophies at War, 128

~

O Holy Spirit, guide all parents to train their children to live according to Christ's new way of living.

Good Desires

All the yearnings we have for good are the crying out of the soul for God under the influence of His love for us.

The True Meaning of Christmas, 11

~

May all my good desires draw me to loving you,
O God.

Opening to God

No soul ever fell away from God without giving up prayer. Prayer is that which establishes contact with Divine Power and opens the invisible resources of heaven. However dark the way, when we pray temptation can never master us.

Characters of the Passion, 12

~

I open myself to you, Lord. Let me dwell in your holy presence every day.

Knowing Christ

Many there are who know Christ as a genial preacher of good fellowship, or as a social reformer of humanitarian leanings, but few there are whoever find him as God among men, the Light and the Life of the world.

The Eternal Galilean, 19

~

I acknowledge you, Lord Jesus, as God-with-us. Let your light shine in my mind.

Love Elevates Us

Love is not subjective, but objective; it is nourished not on fear of being unloved by one who does not get what he wants, but rather by a desire to encourage that person to develop himself to the highest reaches of his personality.

Children and Parents, 13

Grant, Lord, that I may be surrounded by people who love me and raise me to the height of my potential.

The Creative Power of Thoughts

A character is made by the kind of thoughts a man thinks when alone, and a civilization is made by the kind of thoughts a man speaks to his neighbor.

Old Errors and New Labels, 11

I set my mind on spiritual realities, Lord, so that thinking right will help me live well and influence my neighbors for good.

Authentic Prayer

The Holy Hour in our modern rat race is necessary for authentic prayer. Our world is one of speed in which intensity is a substitute for lack of purpose; where noise is invoked to drown out the whisperings of conscience; where talk, talk, talk gives the impression that we are doing something when really we are not; when activity kills self-knowledge won by contemplation.

Those Mysterious Priests, 187–188

I want to give you prime time daily in adoration, Lord, so that you can show me your purpose for my life.

Two Ways to God

There are two ways of knowing how good God is: one is never to lose Him; the other is to lose Him and find Him again.

Thinking Life Through, 80

~

Lord God, you have been so good to me. Grant me the grace always to be faithful to you.

The Power of Love

God loves everybody, not because everybody is lovable—but because He puts some of His own love in every person. That, in essence, is what we have to do: put some of our love in others.

Then, even an enemy becomes lovable.

The Power of Love, 9

Just as you put your love in me, O Lord, help me to make others lovable by putting my love in them.

Cherishing Life

The first deep-seated yearning ... in the human heart is the yearning for *Life*. Of all our treasures it is that which we surrender last, and with the greatest reluctance. Titles, joys, and wealth, power, ambition, honor—all of these we will let go provided we can hold on to that precious, palpitating, vibrating thing called life.

The Divine Romance, 3–4

O God, I thank you for creating me and giving me life.

Christian Optimism

The pagan must always be the pessimist, for he must always feel that this life is too short to give a man a chance, and the Christian will always be the optimist, for he knows that this life is long enough to give a man a chance for eternity.

Moods and Truths, 12

Lord, you have given me the opportunity for eternal life with you, and I seize it every day.

The Unsinkable Church

Every now and then the very life seems to have gone out of the Church, she is pallid with death; her blood seems to have been sapped out of her; her enemies seal the tomb, roll a stone in front of her grave, and say: "The Church will never rise again!" But somehow or other she proves them wrong, she does rise again.

The Divine Romance, 95

Thank you, O Lord, that even in the midst of the worst trials you protect and preserve your Church.

Unselfish Love

St. Thérèse wanted everything to be simple. So she really had two rules. One was never to seek the satisfaction of the self, and secondly, to do everything, to bear everything out of love.

St. Thérèse: A Treasured Love Story, 38

Lord Christ, give me the grace I need to spend myself in loving service of others.

Childlikeness vs. Childishness

Childlikeness is not childish. To be childish is to retain in maturity that which should have been discarded at the threshold of manhood. Childlikeness, on the contrary, implies that with the mental breadth and practical strength and wisdom of maturity, there is associated the humility, trustfulness, spontaneity, and obedience of the child.

On Being Human, 173

~

Lord, as I mature in the Christian life, grant that I may always conduct myself as your child.

God, the Art Restorer

The Heavenly Father in His divine mercy willed to restore man to his pristine glory. In order that the portrait might once more be true to the Original, God willed to send to earth His Divine Son according to whose image man was made, that the earth might see once more the manner of man God wanted us to be.

The Seven Last Words, 49–50

Father, please send the Holy Spirit to restore me in your image and make me the person you want me to be.

Exposing the Devil

The devil's logic is simple: if there is no heaven, there is no hell; if there is no hell, then there is no sin; if there is no sin, then there is no judge; and if there is no judgment, then evil is good and good is evil.

Light Your Lamps, 13–14

~

Our Father in heaven, deliver us from the evil one.

Giving Oneself

All love . . . implies generation: the giving not of what one has, but the giving of what one is.

Love One Another, 12

~

O God, I give myself, all that I am, to you. Receive me and help me give myself in love to others.

When a Meek Person Fights

The meek person is not one who refuses to fight, nor someone who never becomes angry. A meek person is someone
who will never do one thing: he will never fight when his
conceit is attacked, but only when a principle is at stake.

The Cross and the Beatitudes, 15

~

*May I always keep my strength under control, Lord,
and fight only in defense of you and your truth.*

Personal Renovation

No manner of economic or political readjustment can possibly save our civilization; we can be saved only by a renovation of the inner man, only by a purging of our heart and souls, for only by seeking first the Kingdom of God and His justice will all these other things be added unto us.

The Prodigal World, 1–2

Renew me from within, Lord, so that I can act in ways that contribute to the reform of society.

The Appearance of Goodness

Many a tree as it stands in the forest looks fair, fine, solid and valuable, but when it is cut down and sawed for use reveals rottenness, cross grain and knots. Social conformity to low standards may give the appearance of goodness, but in the judgment of God the true character is revealed.

Guide to Contentment, 44

Grant, Lord, that I may always conform to your standards so that I might grow in holiness.

God's Chosen

His Mother was not like ours, whom we accepted as something historically fixed, which we could not change; He was born of a Mother whom He chose before He was born. It is the only instance in history where both the Son willed the Mother and the Mother willed the Son.

The World's First Love, 19

Just as you chose Mary as your Mother, you have chosen me as your disciple. I rejoice in your love for me.

Good and Angry

Not all anger is sinful, for there is such a thing as just anger. The most perfect expression of just anger we find in Our Blessed Lord's cleansing the Temple.

The Seven Capital Sins, 1

~

I promise, Lord, with your help to control my anger
and use it only in defense of what's right.

Christ Meets Our Needs

Our Lord did many things with His human nature, but they are all reducible to three: He taught, He governed, He sanctified. These three offices are related to three principal needs of man if he is ever to be reborn: the need for truth, the need for authority, the need for forgiveness.

Those Mysterious Priests, 79

I thank you, Jesus, that you care for me, and I want you to teach, govern, and sanctify me.

Cultivating Capacity for Heaven

Let no one think he can be totally indifferent to God in this life and suddenly develop a capacity for Him at the moment of death. Where would the capacity for heaven come from if we have neglected it on earth?

The Seven Capital Sins, 72

~

I long for you, Lord, with all my heart, and I look forward to being with you forever.

Sins of Omission

Our greatest sins perhaps have not so much been sins of commission, but sins of omission—the sin of not loving—the sin of which no one ever accuses himself.

Light Your Lamps, 88–89

Have mercy on me, Lord, for I often fail to love others.

The Right Choice

Man can choose between an earthly love to the exclusion of Divine Love, or he can choose a Divine Love which includes a healthy, sacramental earthly love. Either he can make the soul subject to body, or he can make the body subject to the soul.

Peace of Soul, 22

~

Lord God, I love you with all my heart, all my mind, and all my strength.

The Spirit Flows Freely

The Spirit of God is free and always acts freely. His movements cannot be anticipated by any human calculations. One cannot tell when grace is coming or how it will work on the soul; whether it will come as a result of a disgust with sin, or a yearning for a higher goodness.

Life of Christ, 89

Come, Holy Spirit, stir your graces in me and flow through my being—cleansing, nourishing, and strengthening me.

A Ladder to Heaven

The Cross is not a roadblock on the way to happiness; it is a ladder up which one climbs to a heaven of love.

Three to Get Married, 185

~

Lord Jesus, may embracing my cross help me to happiness with you in heaven.

A Sound Conscience

A sound conscience stands firm, no matter whether we dislike its findings, and no matter whether those around us are opposed to them or not.

Lift Up Your Heart, 13

~

Examine me, O God, and help me to make choices always to do what is right.

Reasons God Delays Answers

One is that the delay is for the purpose of deepening our love and increasing our faith; the other is that God is urging us. God may defer for some time the granting of His gifts, that we might the more ardently pursue not the gift, but the Giver. Or we may be asking Him for something He wants us to learn we do not need.

Lift Up Your Heart, 217

Lord, I want your will to be done for me and wait patiently for your answers to my prayers.

Encounter and Care

It has been said that happiness is a twin, which means that we are really never happy unless we share. . . . Man cannot exist without Encounter or without Care, which is a responsible being reacting to others, thus helping others to grow and develop.

Footprints in a Darkened Forest, 102

~

May I find happiness, O God, in meeting others and sharing with them.

A Person's Value

Nowhere is the dogma of the worth of a man better pre-
served and practiced than in the family. Everywhere else
the man may be reverenced and respected for what he can
do, for his wealth, his power, his influence, or his charm,
but in the family a person is valued because he *is*. Existence is *worth* in the home.

Three to Get Married, 114

~

*Lord, may I relate to everyone in my family and
among my friends in a way that makes them feel
valued.*

Intimate with Christ

Christ has not left us orphans; He is with us and more intimately than we are with ourselves. He is still living in the world, moving amongst its poor, instructing the ignorant, comforting the doubtful, and healing the souls of men. Such is His Mystical Life in the Church.

The Mystical Body of Christ, 26

I am delighted, O Christ, to know that you are in the Father; I am in you, and you are in me.

A One-Dimensional Universe?

Formerly, man lived in a three-dimensional universe where, from an earth he inhabited with his neighbors, he looked forth to heaven above and to hell below. Forgetting God, man's vision has lately been reduced to a single dimension, namely, that of his own mind.

Go to Heaven, 2

May I never forget you, O God, and keep my mind fixed on spiritual realities.

The Promise of Tribulation

To have accepted Christ as our righteousness and to have embraced His holy faith is no guarantee of freedom from trials. The Divine Savior never said to His apostles, "Be good and you will not suffer"; but He did say: "In this world you shall have tribulation."

Go to Heaven, 51

Whatever suffering comes, be with me, Lord, and support and strengthen me.

Sacrificial Love

The greatest joys of life are purchased at the cost of some sacrifice. No one ever enjoys good reading, good music, or good art without a certain amount of study and effort. Neither can one enjoy love without a certain amount of self-denial.

Three to Get Married, 176

Jesus, you laid down your life out of love for me; may I also lay down my life for love of my friends.

Twice Born

Grace divides the world into two kinds of humanity: the once born, and the twice born. The once born are born only of their parents; the twice born are born of their parents and of God. One group are what might be called natural. The other, in addition to having nature, share mysteriously in the divine life of God.

Your Life Is Worth Living, 177

Thank you, Lord, for the grace that elevated me to a supernatural life—may I learn to live it to the full.

A Tête-à-Tête with the Lord

Silence in the [Holy] Hour is a tête-à-tête with the Lord. In those moments, one does not so much pour out written prayers, but listening takes its place. We do not say: "Listen, Lord, for Thy servant speaks," but "Speak, Lord, for Thy servant heareth."

Treasure in Clay, 191

Speak to me in the silence, Lord; I want to listen to what you have to say to me.

Awareness of Guilt

The nearer Christ comes to a heart, the more it becomes conscious of its guilt; it will then either ask for His mercy and find peace, or else it will turn against Him because it is not yet ready to give up its sinfulness.

Life of Christ, 41

Be merciful to me, O God, for I know that I have greatly offended you.

A Divine Urge

There is a Divine urge toward life, which is behind every meal, a love behind every sex drive, a truth which pushes the scientist into the laboratory and beyond.

Guide to Contentment, 58–59

~

You have given me a human life, Lord, and I celebrate it every day and in every way.

Simple Wisdom

From the beginning Our Blessed Lord has been found only by two classes: those who know and those who don't know. Divinity is so profound that it can be grasped only by the extremes of simplicity and wisdom.

The Eternal Galilean, 19

I am grateful that I have come to know you, O Lord, and I want to know you more.

Holiness Right Where You Are

The way of St. Thérèse is easy. It's living the life that you are living now, only making it holy. You sacramentalize it.... Your house work, your office work, whatever you happen to do, that's where you start to be a saint. There.

St. Thérèse: A Treasured Love Story, 55–56

O Christ, may I make every aspect of my life holy by doing all things out of love.

Diagnosis of the Soul

Some people are afraid ever to look into their consciences, for fear of what they may find; they are like the other cowards who dare not open telegrams because they dread bad news. But introspection is to the soul what diagnosis is to the body—the first necessary step toward health.

Go to Heaven, 132–133

O God, diagnose the condition of my soul and prescribe for me your therapy for my spiritual health.

Accepting Calvary

If the Father did not spare the Son, and the Son did not spare His Mother, then even the unexplained things of life fit into the Divine Plan. Relief does not always come in harmonious acceptance of Calvary, but peace does.

Those Mysterious Priests, 109

God, I don't always know why bad things happen, but I know you allow them for a reason.

Imagining Our Superiority

Pride is an inordinate love of one's own excellence, either of body or mind or the unlawful pleasure we derive from thinking we have no superiors.

The Seven Capital Sins, 37

~

I humble myself before you, Lord, and put the interests of others ahead of my own.

The Obedience of the Child Jesus

The only recorded acts of Our Blessed Lord's childhood are acts of obedience—to God, His Heavenly Father, and also to Mary and Joseph. He thus shows the special duty of children and of youth to obey parents as the vice-regents of God.

The World's First Love, 105

~

O God, I want to obey you as simply and directly as Jesus obeyed Mary and Joseph.

The Peace of Christ

Our Lord offers a peace and consolation that he alone can confer, a peace that comes from the right ordering of conscience, from justice, charity, love of God and love of neighbor.

The Cross and the Beatitudes, 76

Prompt me, O God, to always do the loving and just thing so that I may rest in your peace.

The Annunciation to Mary

The mystery of the Incarnation is very simply that of God's asking a woman freely to give Him a human nature.... Through the angel, He was saying: "Will you make Me a man?" As from the first Adam came the first Eve, so now, in the rebirth of man's dignity, the new Adam will come from the new Eve.

The World's First Love, 32

~

Give me the grace, O God, to freely say yes to you as Mary did.

The Meaning of Bethlehem and Calvary

God had to come down from heaven to earth to make it right.... Once a soul begins to realize that the world is rotten because it has broken the moral law of God, it has taken the first step toward conversion. God and the soul can meet on the roadway of a broken and disordered world. Such is the meaning of Bethlehem and Calvary.

Love One Another, 53

O God, I turn away from my moral failures and turn to you in repentance.

Desires Direct Us

Desire is to the soul what gravitation is to matter. When we know our desires, we know the direction our soul is taking. If desire is heavenly, we go upwards; if it is wholly earthly, we go downwards.

Way to Inner Peace, 19

~

Lord Christ, you are my heart's desire, and I desire all that you want for me.

The Sacrament That Changes the World

There is no institution in the world so effectively working for social reform as the Church through the confessional, and this for the double reason that the confessional gets at the intention which inspires the act, and reforms the group by reforming the individuals which make up the group.

Moods and Truths, 52–53

I confess my sins to you, O God, so that by reforming my life I may contribute to reforming the world.

Rehearsals for the Big Ones

Unless we can bear up under the trifling trials, we go down under the great ones. When the small heartaches of the day are dignified by the thought of a Divine Purpose in them, then when the great trials come, they will have the Divine Image stamped on them.

The Power of Love, 62–63

Lord, I surrender to you, accepting whatever you allow to happen as a part of your Divine Plan.

Pruned by the Cross

As a tree bears more fruit by pruning, so does man bear
more fruit through the imprint of the Cross.

Thinking Life Through, 175

*Lord, I ask you to cut away my evil inclinations so
that, like a tree that has been pruned, I may bear
more fruit.*

Mary Visits Elizabeth

On hearing the woman's greeting, the child whom Elizabeth bore within her "leaped in her womb." The Old Testament is here meeting the New Testament: the shadows dissolve before the substance. All the longing and expectations of thousands of years as to Him Who would be the Savior are now fulfilled in this one ecstatic moment when John the Baptist greets Christ, the Son of the Living God.

The World's First Love, 40

Lord Jesus, as Elizabeth greeted Mary and as John recognized you while in the womb, may I recognize you in others and welcome them with hospitality.

Religion Without a Cross

The modern man who is not living according to his conscience wants a religion without a Cross, a Christ without a Calvary, a Kingdom without Justice.

Preface to Religion, 148

~

*Lord, help me to shape my conscience on your Truth
and give me the fortitude to follow it.*

Loss of Faith in God and Humanity

As men lose faith in God, they become selfish, immoral and cruel. As men lose faith in Divinity, they lose faith in humanity.

Preface to Religion, 195

~

Increase my faith in you, O Lord, that I might grow in my love for my brothers and sisters.

Breaking the Death Barrier

The only answer to the mystery of death would be for someone to break the death barrier, as we have broken the sound barrier, so that, as sound and fury are left behind in speed, so death would be left behind in newness of life. Someone must pierce the mystery from within. Man could lift his hands in protest against heaven, unless in some way God tasted death.

Footprints in a Darkened Forest, 60

Lord Jesus, I celebrate your victory over death with great joy and thank you for your gift of eternal life.

Sin Condemned Itself

Coming among sinful men, He allowed all their sins to come to a head and to do its worst against Him, namely, put Him to death. Sin could do no more. But in attempting to kill God, which is the nature of sin, sin really wrote its own condemnation on the pages of history.

Philosophies at War, 61

~

Lord Jesus, I repent of my sins and thank you for destroying the power of sin on the cross.

Rebirth to New Life

The Resurrection of the Lord was not the resumption of an old life; it was the beginning of a new life. It was the lesson of Christmas all over again, namely, the world will be saved not by social recovery, but by rebirth—rebirth from the dead by the Power of Divinity in Christ.

The Prodigal World, 155

How wonderful it is, Lord, to live the new life I received from you at my baptism.

Christ's Social Body

Jesus reminded his disciples over and over again that after His Resurrection He would assume another body, not a body like the one which He took from the Blessed Mother, but rather a kind of social body which would be made up of all those who became incorporated into His Kingdom.

The Divine Romance, 63

I am delighted, Lord Jesus, to be part of your new, post-Resurrection social body—the Church.

Unconditional Love

Liking is reciprocal, but loving is not necessarily reciprocal. The friends we say we like, like us. But a mother can love a wayward son even though he does not return the affection. God can love us even when we spurn His graces.

The Power of Love, 19

⁓

O God, thank you for loving me unconditionally, even when I turned away from you.

Following the Truth

It is easy to find truth; it is hard to face it, and harder still to follow it. Modern education is geared to what it calls "extending the frontiers of truth," and sometimes this ideal is prized and used to excuse men from acting on old truths already discovered.

Go to Heaven, 14

Lord, I embrace the truths you have revealed and commit myself to follow them.

Heavenly Blessings

Heaven is a place where we find in its plenitude those things which slake the thirst of hearts, satisfy the hunger of starving minds, and give rest to unrequited love. Heaven is the communion with perfect Life, perfect Truth, and perfect Love, God the Father, God the Son, and God the Holy Spirit to whom be all honor and glory forever. Amen.

The Divine Romance, 27–28

O God, I long for the blessings of heaven, which I already anticipate by my union with you.

God's Anxiety

God is more anxious to save us than we are to save our-selves.

The Seven Last Words, 17

~

Lord, I abandon the temptation to rely on myself and surrender to you, my Savior.

Three for Redemption

In the divine economy of the Redemption, the same three things which cooperated in our fall shared in our redemption. For the disobedient man Adam, there was the obedient man Christ; for the proud woman Eve, there was the humble Virgin Mary; for the tree of the garden, there was the tree of the Cross.

The Seven Last Words, 50

I am grateful, O God, for your marvelous plan that redeemed me from my disobedience and sin.

Window on the World

The natural world is not opaque like a curtain; it is transparent like a window. It reveals God, as a building reveals the architect and as a painting reveals the artist.

The Cross and the Crisis, 74

~

I respond with faith and love to you, Father, as the beauty of your creation reveals you to me.

The Two Philosophies

There are only two philosophies of life: one, the pagan; the other, the Judaic-Christian. In all pagan religions man tries to climb to God. In the Judaic-Christian tradition, God comes to man: by revelation to the prophets for the Jews, in the flesh for the Christians in the person of Jesus Christ the Son of God.

The True Meaning of Christmas, 7

I thank you, Lord Jesus, for faithfully pursuing me until I let you find me.

An Active Virtue

Peace is not a passive but an active virtue. Our Lord never said: "Blessed are the peaceful," but "Blessed are the Peace-makers."

For God and Country, 87

~

Please show me, O Holy Spirit, how to bring peace to all of my relationships.

Jokes for Christ

True followers of Christ, be prepared to have a world make jokes at your expense. You can hardly expect a world to be more reverent to you than to Our Lord. When it does make fun of your faith, its practices, abstinences, and rituals, then you are moving to a closer identity with Him who gave us our faith.

Characters of the Passion, 61–62

No matter what people say about me or to me, I will live my life for you, Lord.

A Happy Sacrifice

The truth gradually emerges that our highest happiness consists in the feeling that another's good is purchased by our sacrifice; that the reason why our pain is bitter is because we have no one to love and for whom we might suffer.

The Eternal Galilean, 185

~

God, when I experience suffering, I will offer it as prayer for someone in need.

Evangelizing Teens

No one will ever convince teenagers by argument that they should know God and their souls. But let them go out and love the poor, the great unwashed, the sick, and they will find God and their souls.

Children and Parents, 63

~

Lord, I pray that the teens I know will find you in their service of the poor and the sick.

Holy Intolerance

Tolerance applies only to persons, but never to truth. Intolerance applies only to truth, but never to persons. . . . Tolerance applies to the erring; intolerance to the error.

Old Errors and New Labels, 105

~

O God, I respect all women and men, but I reject all wrong and harmful ideas.

A Taste of Divine Love

God meant us to take every fine human love as a foretaste of Infinite Love, and if the human heart thrills us, so much more should the Divine Heart set us aflame.

Lift Up Your Heart, 39

~

Lord, may every one of my loves give me a foretaste of your wondrous love.

The Church's Life Principle

Our salvation is from the beginning to the end a progressive incorporation into a supernatural society of human souls. The Church is one body. It is a society of individual baptized souls diverse in function, but moved and vivified by one common life principle or soul, the Holy Spirit.

The Cross and the Crisis, 72

Come, Holy Spirit, and lead me in using my gifts as a member of Christ's Body.

Confessing in Secrecy

The sin confessed is not broadcast, but locked in the secret storehouse of God, and because the institution of confession is surrounded by inviolable secrecy and thus freed from the ravages of publicity, the act of confession is not designed to discourage the sinner.

Moods and Truths, 44

Jesus, when I confess my sins to you in the Sacrament of Reconciliation, I leave encouraged to live a good life.

Every Crisis, an Adventure

As Christians we must realize that a moment of crisis is not a moment of despair, but of opportunity.

Light Your Lamps, 21

~

Lord, may I turn every crisis into an adventure in holiness.

Knowing God's Secrets

I can know something of the existence of God, something of His Infinite Power, Life, and Beauty by contemplating His universe, but I could never divine anything of His secret Thought and Love unless He told me. His creation gives but dim hints of these.

Love One Another, 12–13

God, I listen for your words of encouragement and love.

Actions and Reactions

Unless there is an action there can never be a reaction; unless we give, it shall not be given to us; unless we love, we shall not be loved; unless we pardon evil, our evil shall not be forgiven; unless we are merciful to others, God cannot be merciful to us.

The Cross and the Beatitudes, 31

Father, I forgive all who have offended me, and I welcome your mercy for me.

For a Better World

The truly good man feels the world is the way it is because in some way he has not been better. The keener the moral sensitiveness, the greater is the compassion for those languishing under a burden.

Go to Heaven, 48

May my acts of kindness, O Christ, make my world a little better.

The Assassin of Love

Envy is sadness at another's good and joy at another's evil. What rust is to iron, what moths are to wool, what termites are to wood, that envy is to the soul: the assassination of brotherly love.

The Seven Capital Sins, 13

~

Lord, may I always rejoice in the good and accomplishments of others.

The Victim Priest

Here is the answer as to how Our Lord differs from all the other priests—pagan and Jewish. *All other priests offered a victim distinct from themselves; a goat, a lamb, a bullock, but Christ offered Himself as a victim.* "He offered Himself without blemish to God, a spiritual and eternal sacrifice" (Hebrews 9:14).

Those Mysterious Priests, 18

Thank you, Lord Jesus, for your eternal sacrifice that ransomed me and gave me a share in your divine life.

Obliged to Care

The powerful are always under obligation to the weak. Advantage of any kind is not a personal possession but a trust.

Way to Inner Peace, 33

~

May your great generosity to me, O Lord, prompt me to be generous to others.

The Source of Anxiety

The anxiety underlying all modern man's anxieties arises from his trying to be himself without God or from his trying to get beyond himself without God.

Peace of Soul, 18

I entrust all my concerns to you, Lord, for your love cures my anxiety.

God's Hope

Our Blessed Lord was hopeful about humanity. He always saw men the way He originally designed them. He saw through the surface, grime, and dirt to the real man underneath. He never identified a person with sin. . . . Just as every mother sees her own image and likeness in her child's face, so God always saw the divine image and likeness beneath us.

Your Life Is Worth Living, 69

Lord God, look deep within me to see the person you designed me to be and renew me in your image.

Honoring Mary

There is, actually, only one person in all humanity of whom God has one picture and in whom there is a perfect conformity between what He wanted her to be and what she is, and that is His Own Mother.

The World's First Love, 17

~

Hail Mary, full of grace, the Lord is with you. . . .

The Loneliness of Independence

Modern man is in flight, he wants to live his own life, be his own judge, his own creator, his own savior, but the more he makes himself absolute and independent, the more lonely and frightened he becomes.

Footprints in a Darkened Forest, 257

~

Lord, my whole being relies on you and your promises.

The Blessing of Children

A marriage need not have children to be a Divinely blessed marriage, for children depend on the will of God, cooperating with the husband and wife.

Three to Get Married, 109

O God, I intercede for infertile couples that you will bless them with children or comfort them with your peace.

Spending Time with God

The Holy Hour is not a devotion; it is a sharing in the work of redemption. In the Garden ... Our Lord asked: "Could you not watch one hour with Me?" In other words, He asked for an hour of reparation to combat the hour of evil, an hour of victim union with the Cross to overcome the anti-love of sin.

Treasure in Clay, 188

~

Lord Jesus, I accept your invitation to spend time with you, embracing the good and fighting evil.

The Divine Invasion

God enters the soul like a thief in the night—we may choose whether to welcome Him or to reject Him, but we cannot *prevent* Him from invading the soul that He has made. As the sun rises without asking permission of the night, so Divine life invades us without consulting the darkness of our minds.

Go to Heaven, 19

I invite you, Lord Christ, to invade my being whenever you want, and I welcome you into my heart.

Irrelevant Religion

Religion, like the Prodigal Son, is indeed in a foreign land when it is more interested in mental hygiene than in the forgiveness of sin; in politics rather than prayer; in the theory of relativity rather than in the Absolute; in crime prevention rather than morals; and in sex rather than God.

The Cross and the Crisis, 15

~

Father, you are my God and I belong to you; I pray that you would draw me nearer.

And Then There Were Three

Marital love is happiest when it becomes an earthly Trinity: father, mother and offspring, for by filling up the lacking measure of each in the store of the other, there is built up that natural complement wherein their love is immortalized in the offspring.

Philosophies at War, 136

Lord, may married couples everywhere honor their vows and welcome children into their families.

Choosing Divine Life

God, having made man free, will not destroy his freedom.
There will be no confiscation of humanity by Divinity. If
man is ever to be taken up into the Divine Order there
will have to be a free act on the part of man.

The True Meaning of Christmas, 14

~

*I thank you, Lord, for giving me a share in your divine
life. May I live it more fully.*

Busy About Many Things

Most souls still feeling the necessity of doing something for God and the Church turn to the solace of activity. Instead of going from prayer to action, they neglect prayer and become busy about many things. It is so easy to think we are doing God's work when we are only in motion or being fussy.

Characters of the Passion, 13–14

Lord Jesus, I come into your presence asking that you guide me in my service.

Why Become Childlike?

How can souls find God? It is a psychological fact that it is only by being little that we ever discover anything big. This law raised to the spiritual level tells us how we can find the immense God, and that is by having the spirit of little children.

The Eternal Galilean, 3

O God, I come to you, humbling myself like a child,
so that I can know you and love you more.

Loving the Unlovable

There is no merit in loving others who are lovable. It is easy to love lovable children, but to love them when they are unlovable is the unfailing sign of a family.

Children and Parents, 22

~

Lord, grant me the grace to love and serve people I do not like.

A Healthy Agnosticism

There is ... a sense in which agnosticism is desirable. In fact, a healthy agnosticism is the condition of an increase in knowledge.... Modern agnosticism doubts the things *above* man and hence ends in despair; Christian agnosticism doubts the value of things *below* man and hence ends in hope.

Old Errors and New Labels, 33

~

May valuing the things of earth, Lord, never keep me from knowing and loving you.

The Gift of Peace

True peace is a gift of God; false peace is of our own making. True peace flourishes in an increasing friendship with God; false peace is spawned in forgetfulness of God and exaltation of the self.

Lift Up Your Heart, 14

Thank you, Jesus, for making me your friend and giving me your peace.

Jesus, the Magnet

The Cross and the Ascension, which lifted Christ to heaven, freed Him from all earthly, carnal, and national ties, and enabled Him to exercise universal sovereignty over man. Once crucified, He promised to become a magnet of attraction, drawing all nations and tongues and peoples to Himself.

Those Mysterious Priests, 103

~

Draw me nearer to you, Lord Jesus, and hold me in your embrace.

O Happy Fault!

For all sinners there is hope. If we had never sinned, we never could call Christ Savior.

Thinking Life Through, 80

~

Lord Jesus, I have sinned in my thoughts, in my words,
in what I have done and in what I have failed to do.
All my hope is in you, my Savior.

A Great Exchange

Sanctity is not a question of relinquishing or abandoning or giving up something for Christ; it is a question of exchange.... As I grow in acquaintance with Christ, I find that I can get along without sin, but I cannot get along without His peace of conscience, and so I exchange one for the other.

Moods and Truths, 30

O God, since I want to be a saint, I freely exchange my sinfulness for your peace of conscience.

Christ Died for All

Don't you think ... that Christ was somehow hidden in the six million victims at Auschwitz and Dachau, all those Jews who went to an incinerated death? Though they did not know it and were loyal to the law of Moses even as they understood it, they were in some way continuing unwittingly the Passion of Christ and being saved by it.

St. Thérèse: A Treasured Love Story, 89

Lord, have mercy on all the people who are suffering at the hands of terrorists.

Indifferent to Christ

One can well believe that a crown of thorns and that steel nails were less terrible to the flesh of our Savior than our modern indifference which neither scorns nor prays to the Heart of Christ.

The Seven Last Words, 36

~

Lord Jesus, as you forgave those who crucified you, I pray that you forgive my contemporaries who are indifferent to you. May your mercy draw them.

Urgent Repentance

Christ is at our doors summoning us to repentance, but only those who have religious eyes or ears know how urgent is the task.

Light Your Lamps, 30

~

I hear your call, Lord, and I turn away from my sins and turn to you.

The Necessity of Baptism

The necessity of Baptism as a means of eternal salvation ... is of divine origin. It was Jesus Christ who told us so. Looking back from its revelation to nature, we can see all nature crying out the necessity of Baptism in the sense that it demands a death as a condition of rebirth.

Go to Heaven, 61

I celebrate my baptism, Lord, in which I died to my old self and rose to a new life with you.

Bringing Good from Evil

God would never have given men the power to choose evil if He could not draw goodness out of it.

Love One Another, 31

~

God, please bring good from the evil circumstances of my life.

Strength Under Control

Meekness is the virtue that controls the combative, violent, and pugnacious powers of our nature and is therefore the best and noblest road to self-realization.

The Cross and the Beatitudes, 15

~

Restrain in me, O God, any inclination to engage in fighting with words or actions.

A World Alienated from God

The whole world seems to be in a state of spiritual widowhood, possessed of the harrowing devastation of one who set out on life's course joyously in intimate comradeship with another, and then is bereft of that companion forever.

The Prodigal World, 1

~

Father, may I be a witness to your love for all people of the world.

Led by the Spirit

There is a difference between a man rowing a boat and the same man being driven by a sail full of wind; the soul that lives by the Gifts of the Spirit is swept forward directly by God, rather than by its own reason.

Peace of Soul, 62

Come, Holy Spirit, and lead me in my life and service.

The Church at the Incarnation

The Church was in existence before Peter or James or John or the other apostles became believers. It was in actual existence the very moment when the Word was made flesh and dwelt among us, for at that moment Christ assumed a human nature, the "pattern man," like unto which He would mold us by the fingers of His love and the power of His grace.

The Mystical Body of Christ, 72–73

By your love and grace, O God, shape my life on the pattern of Christ.

Excusing Anger

Why is it that we can find excuses for our anger against our neighbor, and yet we refuse to admit the same excuses when our neighbor is angry with us?

The Seven Capital Sins, 7

When I sin, O God, I will take responsibility for my action and repent.

Two Kinds of Truth

There are two kinds of truth: outer and inner. An *outer* truth is one we master—the distance of the sun from the earth. An *inner* truth is one that masters us—God is merciful to the penitent.

Those Mysterious Priests, 84

May I abide in your word, O Lord, and may it govern my life.

The Power of Desire

Desire is the raw material out of which we fashion either our virtues or vices. As Our Lord said, "Where your treasure is, there your heart is also."

Way to Inner Peace, 19

~

I set my heart on you, O Lord, for you alone are my treasure.

The Secret of Meditation

In the human order a person in love is always conscious of the one loved, lives in the presence of the other, resolves to do the will of the other.... Apply this to a soul in love with God and you have the rudiments of meditation.

God and War, 27–28

Lord, I love you and want to always be aware of your presence.

Occasions of sin

Avoiding the occasions of sin is the easiest way of avoiding sin itself. . . . Environments can make sin repulsive or attractive to us, for our surroundings affect us all. But we can *choose* the environment we wish and can ruthlessly reject the one that leads to trouble.

Go to Heaven, 133

Help me, O God, to avoid environments that lead me to sin.

Heaven's Veterans

There are only war veterans in heaven. No one enjoys its blessedness unless he has fought, for from the first day of creation the Divine command went out that no one should be crowned unless he had struggled.

The Mystical Body of Christ, 275

May all your saints, Lord, intercede for me that I may emerge victorious from my trials.

God's Books

God writes His name on the soul of every man. Reason and conscience are the God within us in the natural order. . . . Men are like so many books issuing from the Divine press, and if nothing else be written on them, at least the name of the Author is indelibly engraved on the title page.

Life of Christ, 26

O God, I belong to you. Claim me and write your name on my soul.

Scripture on Social Morality

No one can pick up the Scriptures without reading a devastating criticism of social moral standards, as when the Divine Savior put a harlot above a Pharisee, a penitent robber above a religious leader, a prodigal son above his exemplary elder brother.

Guide to Contentment, 44

Lord Jesus, I repent of my sins and promise to conduct myself in ways that help others live good lives.

Repressing Egotism

When Our Divine Lord said that the great must be as the least, He made the measure of greatness usefulness and service to one's neighbor in His Name. Service of others is necessary because it involves the constant repression of those egoistic tendencies in us which exult us at the expense of others.

Way to Inner Peace, 86–87

May my generous service of others, Lord, overcome all my selfish tendencies.

The Only Way

If you want to know about God, there's only one way to do it: get down on your knees.

Preface to Religion, 26

~

O God, I kneel in your holy presence seeking to know and love you more.

Excessive Luxury

If there is any indication of the present degeneration of society better than another it is the excess of luxury in the modern world. When men begin to forget their souls, they begin to take great care of their bodies.

The Seven Capital Sins, 51

~

Grant, Lord, that no earthly goods will ever cause me to forget you.

The Power of Mercy

Whenever mercy is confronted not only with pain, but with sin and wrong-doing, it becomes forgiveness which not merely pardons, but even rebuilds into justice, repentance, and love.

The Cross and the Beatitudes, 27–28

Lord, give me the wisdom and grace always to be merciful.

The Fruit of God's Love

Love tends to become like the one loved, and since God loved man, God became man—and this is the Person of Jesus Christ, true God and true man.

Love One Another, 24

~

Lord Jesus, I love you above all and want to become like you in every way.

The Poverty of Secular Wisdom

Do you know any secular University or College in the Western World ... which teaches that man is a creature of God, that this life is a novitiate for the next, that Christ is Redeemer of his soul, that marriage is monogamous, that self-restraint is essential to virtue, and that man ought to save his immortal soul?

Light Your Lamps, 26

Come, Holy Spirit, and grant that I may be truly wise.

A New Humanity

In rising from the dead by the power of God, Christ made the disaster of sin the beginning of its conquest, and the occasion of a new and regenerated humanity under His Headship which is the Kingdom of God.

Philosophies at War, 61

~

Lord Jesus, by the power of your resurrection, destroy the root of sin in me.

Incipient Philosophers

The very first question we asked when we came into this world was the question "Why?", a question which betrays that we are all born incipient philosophers.... We are incurably bent on knowing and discovering the truth of things—that is why we hate to have secrets kept from us.

The Divine Romance, 4–5

~

O God, I want to know the truth about reality and live by it.

A Concurrence of Evils

Just as disease in the body is very often due to a concurrence of bodily weakness with germs that are foreign to the body, so, too, there are evil principalities and powers that concur with the wickedness of man and produce a chaos that is more than human in its origin.

Thinking Life Through, 83

~

Deliver us, Father, from every evil, for the kingdom and the power and the glory are yours forever and ever.

A Bridge to Eternity

God makes everyone run up against a stone wall every now and then in life; on such occasions they feel the crisis of nonentity and have an overwhelming sense of nothingness and loneliness, in order that they may see life not as a city but as a bridge to eternity.

The Power of Love, 80

May I see my trials, Lord, as opportunities preparing me for eternity with you.

Scaffoldings to Heaven

Anyone who lives solely for the world, turning it into an end instead of a means, must end up in cynicism and despair. For creatures cannot give what they promise unless they are used as scaffoldings to the heavenly mansions.

Lift Up Your Heart, 39

Lord, may all the wonderful creatures you have made draw my heart and mind to you.

Charity Produces Unity

Charity ... must be shown to persons, and particularly to those outside the fold who by charity must be led back, that there may be one fold and one Shepherd.

Old Errors and New Labels, 107

Lord, prompt me to show love to others in ways that draw them to you and the Church.

The Universal Law of Life

How does man enter into [the] higher, divine life? The answer is simple; we must follow what would appear to be a universal law. While preserving a complete distinction between nature and grace, we must follow the same law the mineral follows in entering into the plant life and the plant in entering the animal life, namely, *we must die to ourselves.*

Go to Heaven, 58

~

Lord Jesus, I give you my life, dying to myself, so that I can enjoy eternal life with you.

Reflected Beauty

Everything beautiful in the world is a reflection of the Divine Beauty. As Augustine put it, "All that loveliness which passes through men's minds into their skillful hands comes from that Supreme Loveliness, which is above our souls."

Guide to Contentment, 63

O God, in all the beautiful things men and women create, may I see the splendor of your loveliness.

Seeing God Among Us

The more deeply we think about the matter, the more we see that if God is good, we should look for His Way, His Truth, and His Life; not merely to be way, way up there in the heavens, but down here in the dust of our poor lives.

The Eternal Galilean, 74

Lord, I believe that you have come to make your home in me, so I look for you in the events of my daily life.

Beliefs Shape Behavior

Meditation improves our behavior. It is often stated that it makes no difference what we believe, that all depends on how we act; but this is meaningless, for we act upon our beliefs.

Go to Heaven, 159

Lord Jesus, I reflect on you, your life, and your teachings; may my meditations direct my conduct.

What Hell Is Like

Men have spoken of hell in various images but none are more terrible than the image of the silence of God. "... O my God, be thou not silent to me: lest if thou be silent to me I become like them that go down into the pit" (Psalm 28:1).

Characters of the Passion, 53

O God, may I always dwell in your presence and listen as you speak to me.

Undying Love

There are only two words in the language of love: "you" and "always." *You*, because love is unique; *always* because love is enduring. No one ever said: "I will love you for two years and six months." All love songs have the ring of eternity about them.

Three to Get Married, 113

O God, I pray for all married couples that they may enjoy an undying love.

Like Thy Neighbor?

The biblical command is not "Like Thy neighbor," but "Love Thy neighbor." Not every neighbor is likeable, but every neighbor is lovable.

Footprints in a Darkened Forest, 89

~

Lord, give me the grace to perform acts of service and kindness for people I do not like.

Catching Fire

I have found that it takes some time to catch fire in prayer. This has been one of the advantages of the daily [Holy] Hour. It is not so brief as to prevent the soul from collecting itself and shaking off the multitudinous distractions of the world.

Treasure in Clay, 190–191

Lord, I open my heart to you. May it catch fire with your love.

God's Pencil

When we respond to grace we become something like a pencil in the hand. A pencil in the hand, as long as it is directed by the hand, will do anything the hand wants. We are the instruments of God and we obey His will just as the pencil obeys the will of the hand. When there is total obedience there is sanctity.

Your Life Is Worth Living, 172

O God, may your will unfold in me and give your direction to my life.

The Voice of the Spirit

The voice of the Spirit is within the soul; the peace which It brings, the light which It sheds, and the strength which It gives, are unmistakably there.

Life of Christ, 89

Come to me, O Holy Spirit. You are my peace, my light, and my strength.

Everybody Is Tempted

When a person is tempted to evil, he must not think there is anything abnormal about him. A man is tempted, not because he is intrinsically evil, but because he is a fallen man. No individual has a monopoly on temptation; everybody is tempted.

Peace of Soul, 47

~

Give me the strength, Lord Jesus, to resist every temptation.

Making Others Miserable

A happy conscience makes a happy outlook on life, and an unhappy conscience makes us miserable on the inside and everyone else miserable on the outside. When our conscience bothers us, whether we admit it or not, we often try to justify it by correcting others, or by finding fault with them.

Way to Inner Peace, 56

When I'm guilty, Lord, prompt me to go to confession; may I never justify myself by making others miserable.

God's Method

He who does not welcome the Cross, does not welcome Christ. God's method in nature is evolution; God's method in man is Calvary.

Those Mysterious Priests, 109–110

~

Lord God, impress on me the importance and the power of the cross in my life.

The Unteachable Self

Pride is the exaltation of self as an absolute standard of truth, goodness, and morality. It judges everything by itself, and for that reason everything else is a rival, particularly God. Pride makes it impossible to know God. If I know everything, then not even God can teach me anything.

Go to Heaven, 73–74

O God, I renounce pride and all its side effects. And I humble myself before you, submitting to your standards of truth, goodness, and morality.

Mary at Three Births

Mary is present at three births: at the birth of John the Baptist, at the birth of her own Divine Son, and at the "birth" of John the Evangelist, at the foot of the Cross, as the Master saluted him, "Behold thy Mother."

The World's First Love, 40

~

Mary, I honor you as the Mother of God, as the Mother of the Church, and as my Mother.

The Reason for Our Hope

No matter how hopeless things seem to be, there is still hope, for Christ is the Resurrection and the Life. He that can make snowflakes out of dirty drops of water, diamonds out of charcoal, and saints out of Magdalens, can also make you victorious if you but confess Him in His earthly and Mystical Life as Christ the Son of the Living God.

The Prodigal World, 158

Lord Jesus, I place all my hope in you, for you are the Resurrection and my Eternal Life.

The Source of Obedience

Obedience does not mean the execution of orders that are given by a drill sergeant. It springs, rather, from the love of an order and love of Him who gave it.

The World's First Love, 103

Lord God, I love you with all my heart, and I surrender to you.

Unconscious Pride

Pride is the commonest sin of the modern mind and yet the one of which the modern mind is never conscious. You have heard people say: "I like drink too much" or "I am quick tempered," but did you ever hear anyone say: "I am conceited"?

Go to Heaven, 73

Lord, prevent me from unknowingly falling into prideful behavior and grant me the grace to stay humble before you.

Becoming a Christian

To become a Christian does not mean reading religious books, or singing hymns or being kind to neighbors; it means sharing the Divinity that first came to us at Bethlehem.

The True Meaning of Christmas, 26

~

Lord Jesus, thank you for giving me a share in your divine life at my baptism.

True Freedom

The true definition of freedom is the right to do whatever one *ought*, and oughtness implies law, goals, purposes, and perfection. Freedom is a moral power and not a physical one.

Thinking Life Through, 136

O God, grant that I may always freely choose to do the right thing in all circumstances.

The Fear of the Lord

There will never be peace in this world so long as man fears man rather than God. To fear God is not only to love God, but also to love one's fellow man.

For God and Country, 14

~

Lord God, I honor and revere you above all, and may this reverence bear fruit in my life.

Naked Before God

Let each soul stand naked, face-to-face with God in a private audience with Divinity, where spirit meets spirit, so that each man rises from the tryst as a new creature, conscious that he must be worth something since God loves him so!

The Cross and the Crisis, 105

O God, I stand before you totally dependent on you and your love for my worth.

Why People Leave

No one yet has ever left the Body of Christ or His Church for a reason, but many have left for a thing. The thing may differ: it may be pride, wealth, flesh, or the thousand-and-one substitutes for Divinity.

Characters of the Passion, 25

Lord Jesus, I pledge my faithfulness to you and to the Church.

Finding Christ

Only the teachable find the Teacher, only the docile find
the Doctor, only the humble find the Exalted.

The Eternal Galilean, 28

*Lord Jesus, I open myself to you, and I embrace your
word, your teaching, and your way of life.*

Self-Worship

If you do not worship God, you worship something, and nine times out of ten it will be yourself.

Preface to Religion, 17

~

Glory, praise, honor, and worship to you, my Lord and God.

The Limits of Science

Science ... by its very nature, since it deals with facts, tested by facts, can never give us any knowledge about the ultimate with which religion is concerned.

Old Errors and New Labels, 64

~

Lord, grant that by faith I may grow in knowledge of you and your ways.

God's Prodigal Love

God loves us too much to leave us comfortable in our sins.

Lift Up Your Heart, 28

~

Father, forgive my sins and embrace me in your love.

Divine Prompts

Desires are formed in our thoughts and meditations; and since action follows the lead of desires, the soul, as it becomes flooded with divine promptings, becomes less and less a prey to the suggestions of the world.... If a man meditates consistently on God, a complete revolution takes place in his behavior.

Go to Heaven, 160

O Holy Spirit, flood me with your wisdom and strengthen me to resist the world's suggestions.

Supporting Others

Though we cannot love the weaknesses of others, yet we can love the weak and bear their infirmities, not breaking the bruised reed, nor quenching the burning flax.

The Power of Love, 24

Give me the strength, Lord, to help others to bear their burdens.

The Birth of Disbelief

Atheism, nine times out of ten, is born from the womb of a bad conscience. Disbelief is born of sin, not of reason.

Preface to Religion, 27

~

Give me an outpouring of your Spirit, Lord, to protect me from doubt and disbelief.

Overcoming Mediocrity

Most of us settle down to mediocrity. We level off, particularly about middle age. We cannot do that spiritually. We *have* to grow, we *have* to become younger. We *have* to become closer to God.

St. Thérèse: A Treasured Love Story, 50–51

O Lord, renew me in your Holy Spirit and draw me ever nearer.

Invited to Come Dirty

No one else in all the world ever founded a religion wherein a welcome was extended to a sinner, while he was yet a sinner.... All others are merely teachers: they tell us to wash ourselves righteous and then go to God. But He, as a Savior, bids us come dirty that He might have the joy of washing away our sins.

Philosophies at War, 62

Lord Jesus, my Savior, I thank you for cleansing me of my sin.

Christ's Pre-History

Jesus Christ has a pre-history—not to be studied in the rocks of the earth, nor in the caves of man, nor in the slime and dust of primeval jungles, but in the bosom of the Eternal Father.

Love One Another, 19

~

Lord Jesus, I believe that you are in the Father and that I am in you and you are in me.

A World Reborn

Like that world into which Christ was born, the world today needs not a shuffling of old ideas, nor a new economic, not a new monetary system—it needs a New Birth. It needs the intrusion into our order of a new life and a new spirit, which God alone can give.

The Prodigal World, 6

O Holy Spirit, invade our world and bring us an outpouring of your divine life.

The Lost Taboo

Sex today is no longer a mystery, inasmuch as it is currently reduced to a pure biological function. Because its mystery, which is a profound love for another person expressed in corporal unity, has been lost, the taboo in sex has been lost.

Guide to Contentment, 60

~

Lord, I thank you for the gift of sexuality, and I pledge to treat it with respect.

Rampant Envy

Since envy is so rampant in the world today, it is extremely good counsel to disbelieve 99 percent of the wicked statements we hear about others.

The Seven Capital Sins, 20

Set a guard at my ears and mouth, O God, so that I will neither listen to gossip nor start it.

The Climb

Heaven is a city on a hill, hence we cannot coast into it; we have to climb. Those who are too lazy to mount can miss its capture as well as the evil who refuse to seek it.

The Seven Capital Sins, 72

~

I know that heaven comes by your grace, Lord, and I am determined to cooperate faithfully with it.

New Energy for New Life

We must not reconstruct our old life, we must rise to new life. There must be a new energy introduced from without, in the absence of which we must rot in our graves. Christ rose from the dead by the Power of God. It is vain for us to try to rise by any other power. This Life and Power the Risen Savior has given to the Mystical Body, His Church.

The Prodigal World, 155

Lord Jesus, I abandon all self-reliance, and I place my trust in you for the gift of new life.

Surrender

The God-responsive soul thinks of religion in terms of submission to the will of God. He does not look to the Infinite to help him in his finite interests but, rather, seeks to surrender his finite interests to the Infinite.

Peace of Soul, 60

Father, grant that I may love you always, then do with me what you will.

An Intimate Bond

Moses did not command people to believe in him, but to put their trust in the Lord.... Islam demands faith in God..., but not necessarily in Mohammed. But when you come to Christ, here Christianity demands a personal intimate bond. We have to be one with Him. We cannot in any way claim to be Christian unless we reflect the person, mind, will, heart and humanity of Christ.

Your Life Is Worth Living, 31

Lord Jesus, I pray that you would reveal yourself to me more fully and bind me to yourself in an intimate bond.

The Secret of Marriage

Adding to her cooperation with man her cooperation with God, a woman once more affirms the secret of marriage: it takes three to make love; man and woman as a generative principle and God, Who infuses an immortal soul.

Three to Get Married, 148

~

Lord, I pray that married couples will rely on the sacramental grace of matrimony as they bear children and build their families.

An Antidote for Distractions

Meditation allows one to suspend the conscious fight against external diversions by an internal realization of the presence of God. It shuts out the world to let in the Spirit. It surrenders our own will to the impetus of the divine will.

Go to Heaven, 157

Lord God, I come into your presence and subordinate my will to your will.

Christ's New Body

The Church ... is in the truest sense of the term the pro-longation of the Incarnation; it is the new Body which Christ assumes after His Ascension, with which to extend His Kingship throughout the kingdoms of the world; it is the new living instrument through which he teaches, governs, and sanctifies.

The Mystical Body of Christ, 70–71

I celebrate my membership in the Body of Christ, Lord, and want to work with you to extend your kingdom in my world.

The Rock

Christ said that no one could be indifferent to Him.... Whether one believes or disbelieves Him, one is never the same afterward. Christ said that He was either the rock on which men would build the foundation of life, or the rock which would crush them.

Go to Heaven, 49–50

⁓

I believe that you are the Son of God, Lord Jesus. You are the rock foundation of my life.

Joy Within

Pleasure comes from without, but joy comes from within, and it is, therefore, within the reach of everyone in the world.

Way to Inner Peace, 49–50

~

You, Lord, are my joy and my strength. I rejoice in your goodness to me.

The Sacrifice of Christ

Christ the Priest was a Sacrifice from the commencement of His earthly life; in fact, the shadow of the Cross fell across the manger. Being a substitute or a "stand-in" or an Ombudsman, He the just stood for the unjust.

Those Mysterious Priests, 29

I thank you, Jesus, that you offered yourself as ransom for me.

A Bad Exchange

The man who unduly loves riches is a fallen man, because of a bad exchange; he might have had heaven through his generosity, and he has only the earth. He could have kept his soul, but he sold it for material things.

The Seven Capital Sins, 85

Lord, I choose to lose my life, which I cannot keep, so that I may gain heaven, which I cannot lose.

Three Excesses

There are three great passions in man which impel him to excesses in his desire for things that are good. These are *lust*, which the modern world calls sex; *pride* or egotism; and *avarice* or greed, sometimes called security.

Guide to Contentment, 48

Come, Holy Spirit, help me to discipline my passions and keep them in moderation.

The World's in Mortal Sin

The world is in a state of mortal sin and it needs absolution. Vain platitudes about "regeneration," "the Constitution," and "progress" are not going to save us even though we go on shouting them louder and louder. We need a new word in our vocabulary—and that word is God.

The Prodigal World, 42–43

⁓

Father, send the Holy Spirit throughout the world to announce your love and win souls.

The Basis of Peace

The subjection of senses to reason, reason to faith, and the whole man to God as his eternal end and final perfection—that is the basis of peace.

The Cross and the Beatitudes, 73

Lord God, I submit my body, my mind, my soul, and my strength to you.

Reasons for Love

Loving one another is now reasonable, because the God of love made us, the God of love redeemed us, and because the God of love sanctified us.

Love One Another, 11

~

Lord God, thank you for your love. By your grace,
may I grow in loving others as you have loved me.

Becoming Christ-like

The Christian has his fixed goal, namely, to make his life more and more Christ-like. His own nature is like a block of marble and his will is the chisel. He looks out upon his model, Christ, and with the sharp point of his mortifying chisel, cuts away from his nature huge chunks of selfishness, and then by finer and more delicate touches makes the great model appear.

Moods and Truths, 10–11

Show me what I must do, Lord, to cut selfishness from my life and to become more like Christ.

An Empty Christianity

Christianity for some means a vague ethical brotherhood, a broad vacuous grouping of sects, teaching contrary and contradictory versions of Christ's teaching but generally limiting it to social service and good fellowship. This type of Christianity only accepts as much of Christ's teaching as public opinion will approve.

The Cross and the Crisis, 18

Give me the fortitude, Lord Jesus, to honor your name publicly no matter what others may say.

When Everything Is Easy

If one loves, everything is easy; if one does not love, everything is hard.

The Power of Love, 10

Pour out your love in my heart, Lord, so that I may learn to do everything with love.

Wanting the Whole

God gives us little snatches of his goodness in creatures, that we might want the Whole. But some of us want only the swatches and the samples, and not the whole cloth of Divinity.

Lift Up Your Heart, 39

O God, may the snatches of goodness I see in creatures prompt me to desire you, the Creator, entirely.

Thinking Right

The Church asks her children not only to externalize their thoughts and thus produce culture, but also to internalize their thoughts and thus produce spirituality.

Old Errors and New Labels, 10

I meditate, Lord, on you and your teaching so that my thoughts will influence culture and contribute to my spiritual growth.

Permissiveness Is Counterproductive

One of the most serious threats to the relationship between parent and child is permissiveness. Some parents believe that if they do not give their children everything they want, the children will not love them. This may be true for any given moment, but it is not true for life.

Children and Parents, 8

Lord Jesus, bless all parents with the kind of love that enables them to discipline their children.

Simplicity and Wisdom

The simple souls, like the shepherds, find God because they know they know nothing; the really learned souls, like the Wise Men, find God because they know they do not know everything.

The Eternal Galilean, 28–29

I open myself to you, Lord, that you may find me and that I may come to know you better.

The Drama of the Soul

The most interesting drama in all the world is the drama of the human soul. Were it not endowed with freedom, it might go out to war and enterprise alone and unheeded; but master of its choice ... it can use time and things to decide its destiny, its eternity, and its judgment.

Characters of the Passion, 11

Lord God, grant me the wisdom and courage to make the right life choices.

Deserved Chastisement

There is marvelous peace that comes to the soul if all trials and disappointments, sorrows and pains are accepted either as a deserved chastisement for our sins, or as a healthful discipline which will lead to greater virtue.

Way to Inner Peace, 21

I welcome trials and disappointments, O God, as punishment for my sins and as healthful discipline.

Our Prodigal Father

The Prodigal's father was a human example of the Heavenly Father who has given us the gift of freedom, and having given it, refuses to take it away even when we misuse it. No free man can be made good against his will.

The Cross and the Crisis, 2

~

Father, I freely choose to submit my life to you and to obey your commandments.

Mary's Shining Light

The Blessed Mother reflects her Divine Son, without Him she is nothing. With Him, she is the Mother of Men. On dark nights when we are grateful for the moon . . . we know there must be a sun. So in this dark night of the world when men turn their backs on Him Who is the Light of the World, we look to Mary to guide their feet while we await the sunrise.

The World's First Love, 80–81

Blessed among women are you, Mary, and blessed is the fruit of your womb, Jesus.

Faith Brings Certitude

Philosophy gives a proof for the existence of God; the science of apologetics gives the motives for believing in Christ, the Son of God; but all the incontrovertible proofs they offer fall short of the certitude that actually comes to a convert through the gift of faith.

Go to Heaven, 66

~

I believe in you, Father, the Creator of heaven and earth, and I believe in you, Lord Jesus, his only Son.

Be Angry, but Sin Not

Anger is no sin under three conditions: (1) If the cause of the anger be just, for example, defense of God's honor; (2) If it be no greater than the cause demands, that is if it be kept under control; and (3) If it be quickly subdued: "Let not the sun go down on your anger."

The Seven Capital Sins, 2

Holy Spirit, help me to channel my anger into doing the right thing.

Jesus' Desolation

There was a kind of withdrawal of [Jesus'] Father's Face in the terrible moment in which He took upon Himself the sins of the world. This pain and desolation He suffered for each of us, that we might know what a terrible thing it is for human nature to be without God. . . .

The Seven Last Words, 33

Thank you, Lord Jesus, for enduring the absence of your Father, that I may always remain in his presence.

Our Muddled World

The world is not in a muddle because of stupidity of the intellect, but because of perversity of the will. We know enough; it is our choices that are wrong.

Preface to Religion, 33

~

May I make my mark on the world's culture, Lord, by following your will for my life.

Born Again of the Spirit

By being "born again" (see John 3:5) of the Spirit and not of the flesh, we are lifted to the *super*-natural level, one to which we are no more entitled by nature than a rose is entitled to hearing, or a dog is entitled to speech.

Love One Another, 63

I thank you, Lord, for giving me the graces of a super-natural life.

Staying on Target

The intellect builds the target; the will shoots the arrows. One may have a target known to the intellect, but shoot the arrows astray because of a perverse will.

Guide to Contentment, 65

Lord God, may my will always direct me to do what you want me to.

The Model of Humility

By its very nature such undue self-evaluation could be cured only by self-humiliation. That is why He, who might have been born in a palace by the Tiber as befitting His Majesty as the Son of God, chose to appear before men as a child wrapped in swaddling bands.

The Seven Capital Sins, 38

~

Lord Jesus, as you humbled yourself to become a man, I humble myself before you so that I can share more fully in your divine life.

The Way of Tribulation

Since the Cross is the condition of salvation, he who suffers with faith need never ask what is required of him; nor need he spend time wondering whether his task might be somewhere else. If tribulation is the way, then to meet tribulation is a proof that one has not lost the way, but is on the right road.

Those Mysterious Priests, 109

O God, may I embrace all suffering peacefully, recognizing that you are allowing it for a reason.

Supernatural Faith

Faith is a supernatural virtue, whereby, inspired and assisted by the grace of God, we believe as true those things which He revealed, not because the truth of these things is clearly evident from reason alone, but because of the authority of God who cannot deceive nor be deceived.

Go to Heaven, 76

~

Father, I believe what you have revealed to us because you are God and cannot deceive or be deceived.

Transformation in Christ

I keep up the Holy Hour ... to grow more and more into His likeness. As Paul puts it: "We are transfigured into His likeness, from splendor to splendor." We become like that which we gaze upon.

Treasure in Clay, 188

Lord Jesus, I spend time in your holy presence,
wanting to become more and more like you.

Craving God

There is not a single striving or pursuit or yearning of the human heart, even in the midst of the most sensual pleasures, that is not a dim grasping after the Infinite. As the stomach yearns for food and the eye for light and the ear for harmony, so the soul craves God.

Peace of Soul, 53

~

May every desire of my heart, Lord, draw me nearer to you.

Reproductions of Christ

The life of a true Christian is not so much concerned with the avoidance of sin; rather it is an attempt to reproduce in ourselves the life of Christ.

Your Life Is Worth Living, 118

~

Lord Jesus, may I reproduce in my life your character and your ways.

Holding Nothing Back

Intimacy is openness which keeps back no secret and which reveals the heart open to Christ.

Treasure in Clay, 191

~

I unfold my life before you, O Lord, keeping nothing back so that I can be intimate with you.

Love as a Broken Egg

Love is gradually shifting from the center of ourselves to others; what was once a circle is now more like an egg broken open for the manifestation of life.

Footprints in a Darkened Forest, 93

Lord, I break open the love of my heart so that it can bring new life to others.

A Bridesmaid, not a Bride

One of the greatest mistakes the human heart can make is to seek pleasure as a goal of life. Pleasure is a by-product of the fulfillment of duty; it is a bridesmaid, not a bride; it is something that attends and waits on man when he does what he *ought*.

Three to Get Married, 176

O God, may I take pleasure in doing my duty and taking responsibility for the obligations of my life.

Formed by the Church

All misunderstandings come from regarding the Church as an organization. It is not an organization like a club; it is an organism like a body. It was formed not by men coming together into Christ... ; it was formed by the life of Christ *going out* to men.... The Church was not formed by the faithful; it was the faithful who were formed by the Church.

The Mystical Body of Christ, 72

Thank you, Father, for incorporating me into the Body of Christ, where I am being formed as a Christian by the life of Christ.

The Meaning of Freedom

Freedom does not mean the right to do what you please, but the right to do whatever you ought.

Children and Parents, 34

~

I embrace your gift of freedom, O God, and I pledge to use it always to do the right thing.

A Ransom for Our Sin

The purpose of His life, Christ said, was to pay a ransom for the liberation of the slaves of sin; this was a divine "must" that was laid upon Him when He came into the world. His death was offered in payment for evil.

Go to Heaven, 48

~

I thank you, Lord Jesus, for ransoming me from my sins.

The Finger of God

Every demand for the spiritual comes from God, Whose Finger stirs our soul.

The True Meaning of Christmas, 11

~

Come, Holy Spirit, and stir in me the supernatural gifts of faith, hope, and love.

The Forgotten Man

The real problem of our day is the Forgotten Man; ... not the forgotten man who is unemployed, or hungry or economically dispossessed; not *the* forgotten man, but the *forgotten man*—man with a soul, man with a personality, man with duties not only to Caesar but to God, man with a destiny ... in the great brotherhood of the communion of saints where God is love.

The Cross and the Crisis, 64

Lord Jesus, I pray that my family, friends, and neighbors will come to know you and love you.

The Joy of Sacrifice

Love is the only force in the world which can make pain bearable, and it makes it more than bearable by transforming it into the joy of sacrifice.

The Eternal Galilean, 185

~

May love—your love for me, Lord, and mine for you—transform my suffering into joy.

Avoiding Dry Rot

As sin begins with the abandonment of mortification, so conversion implies return to it. The king in *Hamlet* asked, "Can one be forgiven and retain the offense?" There are such things as occasions of sin, namely, those persons, places, and circumstances that dry rot the soul.

Characters of the Passion, 20

Lord, give me the grace to say no to temptations, which draw me away from you.

Possible Saints

Discipline or training is of two kinds—one external, which has to do with the rule, and the other internal, which has to do with reason and conscience. Both are related to obedience. Interior discipline does not so much look to a rule, but to the values which inspired it. It is based upon the fact that everyone is a possible saint.

Children and Parents, 28–29

Lord Jesus, I want to be a saint, so I follow your teaching, your example, and your way of life.

Mary's Intercession

There yet remains to inscribe in our hearts a perpetual love of the Immaculate Heart of Mary, that will express itself daily in such tokens of virtue and love, that on the last day ... we shall hear Him say the most consoling words of all, and the pledge of our eternal salvation: "I've heard My Mother speak of you."

Light Your Lamps, 107

Remember, O most gracious Virgin Mary, that never was it known that anyone who fled to your protection was left unaided.

Life, Love, and Truth

The only reason in the world for loving life and love and truth is because they come from God, and if they do not come from God then there is no good reason for loving them.

Old Errors and New Labels, 89

Father, I thank you for life, love, and truth, which summon me to you.

Taking Sin Lightly

If Our Lord were liberal about our sins and took them lightly, He would never have been sentenced to the Cross.

Lift Up Your Heart, 28

Lord Jesus, I take my sins seriously and work at repenting for them because they sent you to the Cross.

Suffering Begets Love

It is the winds and the winters which try the herbs, the flowers, and the trees; only the strongest survive. Likewise, tribulation tries the soul, and in the strong it develops patience, and patience, in its turn, hope, and hope finally begets love.

The Power of Love, 118

~

May every tribulation that you allow, O Lord,
strengthen me, producing patience, hope, and love.

The Church Rebounds

Christ rose from the dead, not because He is man, but because He is God. The Church rises from the sepulcher in which violent hands or passing errors would inter her, not because she is human, but because she is divine.

The Divine Romance, 100

Thank you, Holy Spirit, for protecting the Church from error and efforts to destroy her.

Being Religious

You can love the lovable without being religious; ... but you cannot love those who hate you without being religious; you cannot atone for your guilty conscience without being religious.

Preface to Religion, 36–37

~

Change my heart, O God, so that by the power of the Spirit I might repent of sin and love others without reserve.

Accepting Christ

As in the beginning, [man] was free to accept God or reject Him, so now in history he is free to accept God's Son, Jesus Christ, or reject Him. The symbol of Christianity for that reason is the Cross, whereunto that Great Figure is nailed. . . . He can only wait for us! But oh! How He waits: arms outstretched to embrace; heart open to love!

Philosophies at War, 62

~

I run to you, Jesus, and ask you to enfold me in your loving embrace.

Mary, Our Mother

It was by weakness and disobedience at the foot of the tree of Good and Evil that Eve lost the title of the Mother of the Living; it is at the foot of the Cross that Mary, by sacrifice and obedience, regained the title of the Mother of Men.

The Seven Last Words, 26–27

Holy Mary, Mother of God, pray for us sinners, now and at the hour of our death.

The Hub and the Spokes

Alienation from self and from one's fellow man has its roots in separation from God. Once the hub of the wheel, which is God, is lost, the spokes, which are men, fall apart. God seems very far away from the modern man; this is due, to a great extent, to his own Godless behavior.

Go to Heaven, 5

Hold on to me, Lord God, and never let me go.

Wanting Everything

St. Thérèse said, "This became the rule of my life. I wanted everything. I wanted to be perfect. I wanted to be God's." You know the only reason we are unhappy, my good people, is because we are not striving enough to be holy as she was, wanting everything.

St. Thérèse: A Treasured Love Story, 54

~

O God, like St. Thérèse, I "want everything"—I want to be holy, a saint.

The Way Out of Chaos

If the Cross ended His life, if His Calvary was a hopeless fight against sin, then the pathos of our misery would be deepened and the riddle of our life darkened. But having met the enemy and overcome the worst, He becomes not only a Savior but a final Authority who can tell us the way out of all the mad chaos of this hour.

Philosophies at War, 61

Jesus, by your victory at Calvary, deliver me from my sins and show me the way out of the chaos in my life.

The Hope in Hopelessness

Since Christ came into this world to bring victory out of defeat, then the more hopeless the situation, the more certainly does the Divine Power operate.

Light Your Lamps, 115

~

When things appear to be hopeless, O God, I expect you to bring me resolution and relief.

The Divine Copier

All the men who have ever lived and will ever live are the raw material awaiting the stamp of the Divine Original. But in order to be like Him, that is, a sharer of His Divine Life, we must be struck off that Die. And the Baptismal Font is the new Bethlehem where the copies are made, for there men are reborn again to the Life of God.

The Prodigal World, 7

Thank you, Father, for my baptism that made me a sharer in your divine life and a copy reborn in the image of your Son.

Deciding Our Judgment

It is not the fear that God is going to judge us some day that is frightening; it is that our daily living is forging the judgment.

Guide to Contentment, 54

~

I conduct my life carefully, God, not only to avoid offending you but also to become more like Jesus, your Son.

Obedience in Threes

Our Lord spent three hours in redeeming, three years in teaching, and thirty years in obeying, in order that a rebellious, proud, and diabolically independent world might learn the value of obedience.

The World's First Love, 104

~

I want to obey you, Lord Jesus, as you obeyed your Father.

An Accurate Self-Estimation

Humility is not an underestimation of our talents or gifts or powers, nor is it their exaggeration. A man who is six feet tall is not humble if he says he is only five feet four inches tall, just as he is not humble if he says he is seven feet tall. Humility is truth or the recognition of gifts as gifts, faults as faults.

The Seven Capital Sins, 44

~

Lord, I present myself to you as your servant and pledge to use well all the gifts you have given me.

When No One Is Watching

The best influences in life are undeliberate, unconscious, when no one is watching, or when reaction to the good deed was never sought.

Way to Inner Peace, 70

~

Whatever good I do, O God, I do it without expecting recognition or praise.

Ultimate Conflict Resolution

The ultimate resolution of all conflicts will not be accomplished until after the Resurrection of the Body, when the bodies of the just who died in the state of grace will reflect and enjoy the beauties of the soul.

Peace of Soul, 47

I believe, Lord, in the resurrection of the body and life everlasting.

Not Enough

It was not enough that the Son of God should come down from the heavens and appear as the Son of Man, for then He would have been only a great teacher and a good example, but not a Redeemer. . . . Teachers change men by their lives; our Blessed Lord would change men by His death.

Life of Christ, 91

I thank you, Lord Jesus, for my baptism in which you allowed me to share in your death bloodlessly so that I might share in your resurrected life.

The Work of the Spirit

The Holy Spirit woos the soul, draws it to closer fellowship, to more intimate union, becomes our Sanctifier just as the Father is our Creator and the Son is our Redeemer. This is one of the fruits of the Spirit in our daily lives.

Your Life Is Worth Living, 117

~

O Holy Spirit, woo me into an intimate relationship with the Father, the Son, and you.

The Church's Intrinsic Sanctity

The scandals or sins of its members do not affect the intrinsic sanctity of the Church. Because our hands are dirty, the whole body is not polluted.

The Mystical Body of Christ, 155

~

May my repentance of sin and my good behavior, Lord, help restore the negative reputation of your Church from scandals.

Prime Time with the Lord

The Holy Hour. Is it difficult? Sometimes it seemed to be hard; it might mean having to forego a social engagement, or rise an hour earlier, but on the whole it has never been a burden, only a joy.

Treasure in Clay, 189

~

Lord God, I promise to be generous in spending prime time with you every day.

Divinized Humanity

The end and purpose of God coming to this earth was to bring us to perfect union with the Father. How could He do this? By showing our flesh is not a barrier to divine intimacy, by taking it up to heaven itself, by showing those who pass through trials, sufferings, misunderstandings . . . that they will have their body glorified.

Your Life Is Worth Living, 108

What a privilege it is, O God, to share in your divine life—thank you for lifting our human natures to heaven.

Mother Mary

Here at last is the answer to the query, "Did Mary have other children besides Jesus?" She certainly did. Millions and millions of them! But not according to the flesh. He alone was born of her flesh; the rest of us were born of her spirit.

The World's First Love, 131

Lord Jesus, thank you for giving me your Mother as my Mother.

Guardian Angels

Every person has a guardian angel, because every person has an immortal destiny and is worth more than the entire universe.

Thinking Life Through, 32

~

O my Guardian Angel, I thank you for protecting me and interceding for me.

Reaching Beyond Ourselves

Men are more anxious for primacy than they are for service. That is why it took Divinity to give this new concept of love. A man must sweep out of himself into a larger world, make himself one with the purposes of God, which is to help the weak and stricken humanity.

Footprints in a Darkened Forest, 92

Lord, bring me opportunities to reach beyond myself to serve people in need.

Evolving New Creatures

One wonders why a world so much given to the philosophy of evolution does not see the grace of Jesus Christ as the answer to its aspirations. . . . There is no emergent in the whole field of evolution comparable to the "new creatures" which emerge from the Sacrament of Baptism. True greatness of life is not a push from below, but a gift from above: "I am come that you may have life and that in abundance."

Go to Heaven, 55–56

~

I rejoice, O God, that you have made me a new
creation and have given me eternal life.

The Eucharistic Community

The first effect of the Eucharist is personal; the second effect is communal and social, inasmuch as the soul is introduced not only to its Maker, but to its brother, in that fellowship of the saints, an organized society of spiritual units where the integrating principle is Love.

The Cross and the Crisis, 106

It is wonderful to me, Lord, that receiving your Body and Blood unites me to many brothers and sisters.

Tuning In

Just as our modern world is bathed in radio and television waves but only those who are tuned in to them receive their messages of knowledge and enjoyment, so, too, there is a radiation through history of this Divine Life, but only those who freely appropriate it ever enjoy its peace and blessing.

The True Meaning of Christmas, 27–28

Speak to me, Lord, for I am listening to you.

The Family Rosary

Married couples ought to say the Rosary together each night, for their common prayer is more than the separate prayers of each. When the child comes, they should say it before the crib, as Joseph and Mary prayed there.

The World's First Love, 100

May our praying the Rosary, O Lord, bring peace to our relationships and to the world.

The Unreliability of Sin

Since pride is a capital sin, it follows that a first condition of conversion is humility: The ego must decrease, God must increase. This humiliation most often comes by a profound realization that sin does not pay, that it never keeps its promises.

Characters of the Passion, 18

Turn, O God, and save me from my sins.

Jesus Knows Us Well

By permitting the Prince of Darkness to tempt Him, even though it was wholly exterior and did not touch His sinless soul, Jesus proved that He is not insensible to our difficulties, our sorrow, and our temptations.

The Eternal Galilean, 55

Lord Jesus, look into my heart and grant me the grace to stay on the road to eternal life with you.

A Little Kindness Is Not Enough

Lift a dew drop from a leaf, and you can never replace it. Evil, in like manner, is too deep-seated in the world to be righted by a little kindness or reason and tolerance.

Preface to Religion, 57

Thank you, Lord Jesus, for coming to earth and over-coming the work of the devil.

Meditation and Character

No thought is born without silence and contemplation. It is in the stillness and quiet of one's own intellectual pastures, wherein man meditates on the purpose of life and its goal, that real and true character is developed.

Old Errors and New Labels, 11

~

O Holy Spirit, flood my thoughts with wisdom that I may act in ways that please you.

God the "Deceiver"

As God is a "deceiver" in making the world point to Him rather than to us, so from another perspective God is a deceiver because at first He seems forbidding; but once He is embraced, He becomes a veritable passion.

Lift Up Your Heart, 40

O God, I am so glad you "deceived" me into finding my way into your loving embrace.

By-products of Union with God

The peaceful soul does not seek ... to live morally, but to live for God; morality is only a by-product of the union with Him. This peace unites the soul with his neighbor, prompting him to visit the sick, to feed the hungry and to bury the dead.

Go to Heaven, 67

~

I am glad to be united with you, Lord, and so to find real peace in the service of the poor and marginalized.

Enticing Us Back

Man's misuse of freedom became for God the occasion of offering Himself as a Holocaust of love, not to force men back to Him, for His hands were nailed, but to entice them back by a revelation of greater love in which He laid down His life for His friends.

Thinking Life Through, 138–139

Thank you, Lord Christ, for laying down your life to bring me back to God.

Which Authority?

The problem confronting the religious man of today is not whether he will obey or disobey law and authority; but, which of the two he will obey, namely, the authority of public opinion, or the authority of Christ and tradition.

Moods and Truths, 84

~

I will obey you, Lord, and I will not be swayed away from your ways by the opinions of others.

Start Now!

You too must strive for perfection, not just go on doing the same things every day, but do them with greater love, greater intensity, bearing things in union with the sufferings of our Blessed Lord, loving your neighbor more, speaking less uncharitably of neighbors, starting now!

St. Thérèse: A Treasured Love Story, 51

Lord Jesus, give me the grace to do even the smallest thing with love.

A Secular Spirit

At first it may seem unfair to characterize our present Western civilization as secular. It may be objected that there are millions of Jews, Protestants and Catholics who are leading lives in close union with God. This, of course, is true. But here we are speaking not of a multitude, but of a spirit; not of numbers, but of influences; not of a minority, but of a temper.

Philosophies at War, 26–27

Father, I reflect on your word so that I might escape the traps of secularism.

God Thirsts

Having poured forth all the waters of His everlasting Love on our poor parched hearts, it is no wonder that He thirsts for love. If love is reciprocal then certainly He has a right to our love. Why do we not respond? Why do we let the Divine Heart die of the thirst for human hearts?

The Seven Last Words, 44

As you poured out your love for me, Lord, I pour out my love for you.

A Test for Love

Love is not "broadmindedness." Capacity for indignation is sometimes a test of love, for there are enormities which true love must not only challenge, but resist.

Love One Another, 32

~

Lord Jesus, give me the discernment and courage to confront and resist wrongdoing.

Losing All to Gain All

If we save our life in this world, we lose it in the next; if we lose our life in this world, we save it in the next. If we sow in sin, we reap corruption; if we sow in truth, we reap life everlasting. But we cannot do both.

The Cross and the Beatitudes, 85

~

Lord, grant that I may lose what I cannot keep in order to gain that which I cannot lose.

Partakers of Divine Life

What God did to that individual human nature which He took from Mary His Mother is what He wills to do, in a lesser degree, to every human nature in the world, namely, to make us partakers of His divine Life.

The Prodigal World, 7

What a marvelous gift, O Lord, that you have given me a share in your divine life!

Enjoying Old Age

The best way to enjoy old age is to see in it a time for making up for the sins that went before, and living in hope for the joys that lie before one. But this takes Faith.

Guide to Contentment, 49

~

May I spend my autumn years, O God, with enough faith to make up for my sins and to live in hope.

Inordinate Pleasures

Lust is an inordinate love of the pleasures of the flesh. The important word here is *inordinate* for it was Almighty God Himself who associated pleasure with the flesh.

The Seven Capital Sins, 25

Thank you, O God, for the blessings of sexuality. May I always regard it with self-control.

United to the Cross

The Passion of Christ prolongs itself consciously in all those who by an act of the will join their frustrations, anxieties, fears, loneliness and sufferings to His Cross. "I have been crucified with Christ; the life I now live is not my life but the life which Christ lives in me" (Galatians 2:20).

Those Mysterious Priests, 109

Lord Jesus, I embrace your cross and unite my sufferings to your passion.

Inclined to Good and Evil

Man has aspirations to good which he finds impossible to realize completely by himself; at the same time, he has an inclination toward evil which solicits him away from his ideals.

Peace of Soul, 38

~

O Holy Spirit, strengthen me to do good and to resist my evil inclinations.

Reparation and Resolution

Because the past is with him in the form of remorse or guilt, because the future is with him in his anxiety, it follows that the only way man can escape either burden is by reparation—making up for the wrong done in the past—and by a firm resolution to avoid such sin in the future.

Go to Heaven, 123

~

Lord, show me how to make reparation for my offenses.

Know, Love, and Serve

Because God is Life, I must serve Him; because He is Truth, I must know Him; because He is Love, I must love Him. Hence the true nature of man is a creature made by God, and destined to know, love, and serve Him in this world and be happy with Him in the next.

The Cross and the Crisis, 68

O God, with all my heart I want to know you, love you, and serve you in this life and be happy with you forever in the next.

Conductivity

Sympathy is a temper or character which draws others together. It is what might be called conductivity. The Greek origin of the word "sympathy" implies "suffering with." It's a kind of silent understanding when heart meets heart.

Footprints in a Darkened Forest, 108

~

Lord, give me a heart to support others who are suffering.

Nature's Vanguard

Each person has only one heart, and as he cannot eat his cake and have it, so he cannot give his heart away and keep it. Jealousy, which has been instinctively inseparable from the beginnings of love, is a denial of promiscuity and an affirmation of unity. Jealousy is nature's vanguard to monogamy.

Three to Get Married, 113

Lord, I pray for all married couples that they may have enough grace and jealousy to remain faithful.

Bad Catholics

It is no great objection against the Mystical Body to urge that some Catholics are bad. The Church no more expected to have perfect Catholics than Our Lord expected to have perfect apostles. Catholics may be bad, but that does not prove that Catholicism is wicked, any more than a few bigots prove America is bigoted.

The Mystical Body of Christ, 156

Holy Spirit, thank you for protecting the Church from the bad behavior of a few and from those who hate her.

The Lord's Day

Remember, Our Lord always spoke of His crucifixion and His sufferings in terms of hour, His glory in terms of day. Evil had its hour, God had His day.

Your Life Is Worth Living, 97

~

I thank you, Christ, that in your hour of suffering and glory, you conquered my sin and my death.

Becoming a Saint

I say to live in these troubled days, we have to become saints. A saint is one who makes Christ lovable. That's the definition of a saint.

St. Thérèse: A Treasured Love Story, 40

~

Lord Jesus, I want to become a saint so that I can spread your love to others.

Redemptive Work

Now with the theology of the Little Flower, your spiritual life will be changed. You will not just be praying for yourselves. You have the world to pray for. You are continuing His redemptive work with the little trials you have to bear. All of these Christ makes use of and says, "I'm suffering through you, and we are redeeming souls."

St. Thérèse: A Treasured Love Story, 93

May every little inconvenience, Lord, be a prayer for persons in the Body of Christ who need prayer the most.

The Power of the Cross

Few of Christ's words or actions are intelligible without reference to His Cross. He presented Himself as a savior rather than merely as a teacher. It meant nothing to teach men to be good unless He also gave them the power to be good, after rescuing them from the frustration of guilt.

Go to Heaven, 35

~

By your death on the cross, Lord Jesus, empower me to live a good life.

The Church and Liberty

The world will not quickly realize that the Church, which it believed was so restraining to liberty, is really the only one that makes us free, and that which was thought so much behind the times is the only institution which has survived the times.

The Cross and the Crisis, 28

I thrive, O God, in your Church, where I find true freedom.

An Impetus for Good

When this Christ-life gets inside us, it affects our intellect, by giving us a truth which reason itself cannot know; it affects our will, by giving us an impetus and an energy for good which we could not produce of and by ourselves.

The True Meaning of Christmas, 26–27

What a treasure you have given me, Lord Christ, by filling my mind and will with your divine life!

Treasure Within

The excessive dedication to luxury and refinement is always an indication of the inner poverty of the spirit. When the treasure is within, there is no need of those outer treasures that rust consumes, moths eat, and thieves break through and steal.

*Characters of the Passion,*15–16

You are my treasure, Lord, and I set my heart entirely on you.

Watching in Silence

Meditation is a more advanced spiritual act than "saying prayers"; it may be likened to the attitude of a child who breaks into the presence of a mother, saying: "I'll not say a word, if you will just let me stay here and watch you."

Go to Heaven, 15

~

As I keep watch in silence, O God, let me sense your holy presence.

Becoming Little

We cannot always be children, but we can always have the vision of children, which is another way of saying we can be humble. And so in the spiritual order the law remains the same: if a man is to discover anything big, he must always be making himself little.

The Eternal Galilean, 6

I make myself little before you, Lord, so that I can discover your greatness.

Representatives of God

Parents in giving commands have this thought in mind: "I ask obedience of you because I am obedient to the Lord and responsible to Him." Then children will understand that in obeying their parents they are obeying the Lord.

Children and Parents, 18

I pray for all children, O God, that by obeying their parents, they will learn to obey you.

Knowing with God

The very word "conscience" means *knowing with*—knowing with Whom but God? For conscience is the impact of Divine Truth and Goodness on our inner self.

Lift Up Your Heart, 13

~

Impress your truth and goodness on my soul, O Lord.

The Sun of Righteousness

As the smallest light beam is but a reflection of the light and heat that are the sun, so all truth and all love have their origin in God.

The Power of Love, 10

~

O God, shine the light of your truth in my mind and inflame my heart with the fire of your love.

Heavenly Helpers

In humanity, it is the person or the individual who has worth, therefore God has provided him with a guardian. To eschew this companionship is to abandon heaven's help.

Thinking Life Through, 32

~

Angel of God, be at my side, to light and guard, to rule and guide.

The Search for Meaning

The quest for God is essentially the search for the full account and meaning of life. And life has a meaning because the essence of God is love.

The Divine Romance, 12

~

Lord, you alone give meaning to my life.

Person-to-Person

Why should a confessor stand between my God and me? For the same reason that the human nature of Christ stands between His divinity and me. If we were angels, there might be a confession of spirit to spirit, but being made up as we are of body and soul it is fitting that a body or a human nature be the means by which we commune with God.

Moods and Truths, 39

I take comfort, Lord Jesus, when I meet you in the confessional in the person of the priest.

Automatic Behaviors

We acquired the bad habits only because we gave ground to them by a consent of the will until they became automatic and perhaps even unconscious. To master them we must reverse the process and use the will to break their automatic functioning.

Go to Heaven, 133

May your grace, O Holy Spirit, activate in my will the strength to break my bad habits.

The Hair Shirts Next Door

What the Little Flower gives us is this supreme lesson in contrast with the past. She is very modern. There is no need of anyone wearing a hair shirt. Our neighbors are hair shirts! Life is a hair shirt! We have to put up with it.

St. Thérèse: A Treasured Love Story, 56

~

Lord Christ, help me to bear all wrongs patiently and to serve those who offend me.

If We Knew . . .

If we knew what a terrible thing sin is and went on sinning; if we knew how much love there was in the Incarnation and still refused to nourish ourselves with the Bread of Life; . . . if we knew all these things and still stayed away from Christ and His Church, we should be lost!

The Seven Last Words, 7–8

O *Christ, I glory in your love and in the nourishment I receive in the Eucharist.*

Liar, Liar . . .

Nowhere in Sacred Scripture do we find warrant for the popular myth of the devil as a buffoon. . . . Rather is he described as an angel fallen from heaven, and as the "Prince of this world" whose business is to tell us that there is no other world.

Light Your Lamps, 13

May I never succumb, Lord God, to doubts that come from the devil.

What's Happening?

If there is no fixed concept of justice how shall men know it is violated? Only those who live by faith really know what is happening in the world.

Light Your Lamps, 11

~

How good it is, God, that by faith in you I can appreciate the invisible spiritual realities that shape the world.

The Wound of an Empty Tomb

God transferred our transgressions, our sufferings, our poverty to Himself and bore them away as the Heavenly Scapegoat. More important still, He overcame them, and He triumphed by overcoming the pain by giving the earth the only serious wound it ever received—the wound of an empty tomb.

Those Mysterious Priests, 55

I am grateful to you, Lord Jesus, for taking my sin and suffering on yourself and overcoming them by your death and resurrection.

Jesus, Meek and Humble

If ever innocence had a right to protest against injustice, it was the case of Our Lord. And yet He extends pardon. Their insults to his Person, He ignores. Had He not preached meekness? Now must He not practice it?

The Cross and the Beatitudes, 17

May I imitate your humility, Lord, when I am belittled or insulted.

Activating God's Mercy

God's mercy is always present. His forgiveness is ever ready, but it does not become operative until we show Him that we really value it.... Pardon is not automatic—to receive it we must make ourselves pardonable. The proof of our sorrow over having offended is our readiness to root out the vice that caused the offense.

Go to Heaven, 125

Lord God, by your grace help me root out the vice that causes me to sin.

The Original

Man was made originally to the Image of God. Now that the image was defaced, who could better restore it than the Original Image according to which he was made? Thus the love that was spurned and rejected now appears in history as a Redeemer.

Philosophies at War, 61

⁓

You, Christ, are my Redeemer. Restore your image in me that I defaced by my sins.

Hiding Behind Externals

There come moments, at night or when alone or in the silence of the country, when we cannot help but pass judgment on ourselves. But those whose consciences are no good avoid this by immersing themselves in externals.

Guide to Contentment, 53

~

In quiet moments, I recognize my sinfulness, Lord, and I repent to keep my conscience clear.

Pleasure and Propagation

God associated pleasure with the marital act in order that husband and wife might not be remiss in their social obligation to propagate humankind and raise children for the Kingdom of God.

The Seven Capital Sins, 25

~

May all married couples, O God, come to value the unitive and procreative purpose of marriage.

Not Suffered Enough

He suffers with us.... It is just this that St. Paul means when he says that we should fill up those things that are wanting to the sufferings of Christ. This does not mean Our Lord on the Cross did not suffer all He could. It means rather that the physical historical Christ suffered all He could in His own nature, but that the Mystical Body of Christ, ... has not suffered to our fullness.

The Prodigal World, 99

~

I take up my cross, O Lord, to contribute my share to the necessary suffering of the Body of Christ.

Elevating Human Nature

When we say that God became Man, we do not mean that the Godhead was cut down to human dimensions; it means, on the contrary, that a human nature was taken up into the Person of God and made One with Him.

The True Meaning of Christmas, 20

~

What a great privilege you have given us, O Lord,
that you have made us one with God!

Our Visited Planet

To turn a man's heart away from perishable things to the eternal values of the soul was one of the reasons for Christ Our Lord's visit to the earth. His teaching from the beginning was not only a warning against covetousness, but a plea for greater trust in Providence.

The Seven Capital Sins, 84

~

I place all my trust in you, O Lord, and ask you to enfold me in your love.

The Most Apples

The chances are that there is a bit of jealousy, a bit of envy, behind every cutting remark and barbed whispering we hear about our neighbor. It is well to remember that there are more sticks under the tree that has the most apples.

The Seven Capital Sins, 20–21

~

Seal my lips, Lord, that I may not judge others on the basis of jealousy or gossip.

A Spiritual Agriculturalist

When anyone instructs you in Christian doctrine, he does not give you faith. He is only a spiritual agriculturalist, tilling the soil of your soul, uprooting a few weeds and breaking up the clods of egotism. It is God who drops the seed.

Go to Heaven, 78

~

Thank you, Lord, for planting the seeds of faith in me.

A Listening Ear

For meditation the ear of the soul is more important than the tongue. St. Paul tells us that faith comes from listening. Most people commit the same mistake with God that they do with their friends: they do all the talking.

Go to Heaven, 158

I open the ears of my mind and heart to you, O Lord.
I want to hear what you are saying to me.

Nourished by God

A man is worth something not only because the God-man died for him, but also because He lived again for him, nourishing him like a mother nourishes her babe, with His own everlasting life.

The Cross and the Crisis, 104

~

Your new life in me, O Christ, nourishes and strengthens me.

It's Hard to Keep a Secret

God created the world for something like the same reason that we find it hard to keep a secret. Good things are hard to keep.... God could not keep, as it were, the secret of His love and the telling of it was creation.

The Divine Romance, 31–32

I stand in awe, Lord, when I realize that you loved me into existence.

A Sublime Transaction

Sanctity, then, is not giving up the world. It is exchanging the world. It is a continuation of that sublime transaction of the Incarnation in which Christ said to man: "You give Me your humanity, I will give you my Divinity."

Moods and Truths, 32

What a marvelous trade you made with me, O Lord, giving me a share in your divinity for a share in my humanity.

A Cooperative, Creative Act

Every descent of new life into the body of a woman is possible only because God infused the soul into the child by a creative act.... Nowhere within creation does God more intimately cooperate with a human than in the generation of life.

Three to Get Married, 110

~

What a wonder, O God, that human beings cooperate with you in creating new life!

The Price of Freedom

The possibility, not the necessity, of moral evil, of wars and social injustices which follow them, is the price we have to pay for the greatest good we possess—the gift of freedom. God could, of course, at any moment stop a war, but only at a terrible cost—the destruction of human freedom.

Love One Another, 34–35

~

I appreciate your wisdom, O God, in that you don't prevent bad things in order to protect our freedom.

Christ the Priest

Would that the world would cease regarding Christ as a teacher and begin to adore Him as a Priest, who brings God to man by the gift of Divine Life, and man to God by the gift of Divine pardon.

The Eternal Galilean, 121

I celebrate your divine priesthood, Lord Jesus, and I thank you for your gift of divine life and pardon for my sins.

Immaculate Mary

If a ship is sailing on a polluted canal and wishes to transfer itself to clear waters on a higher level, it must pass through a device which locks out the polluted waters and raises the ship to the higher position.... Mary's Immaculate Conception was like that lock, ... through her, humanity passed from the lower level of the sons of Adam to the higher level of the sons of God.

Go to Heaven, 31

Immaculate Mary, your praises we sing. You reign now in heaven with Jesus our king.

All for the Kingdom

The poor in Spirit are those who are so detached from wealth, from social position, and from earthly knowledge that, at the moment the Kingdom of God demands a sacrifice, they are prepared to surrender all.

The Cross and the Beatitudes, 49

~

Lord, prepare my heart to offer sacrifices for your kingdom.

Crowding Out Bad Habits

Evil habits are not driven out by our hate of them (for we do not always hate them properly). They are crowded out by our love of something else.... No new, competing love is large enough except the love of God Himself, with all that that love makes us long to do.

Go to Heaven, 134

⌐

May your love fill my heart, O God, and drive out my evil habits.

Discovering Joy

It is one thing to discover one's nothingness and to rest there—that is sadness. It is quite another thing to discover that one is nothing, and from there to make use of the Divine Energies—that is joy.

Way to Inner Peace, 49

Without you, O Lord, I sense my nothingness, but your presence floods me with joy.

A Double Law of Gravitation

In every human being, there is a double law of gravitation, one pulling him to the earth, where he has his time of trial, and the other pulling him to God, where he has his happiness.

Peace of Soul, 18

~

Draw me to yourself, O God, and hold me in your embrace.

The Divine Builder

Everything in space and time exists because of the creative Power of God. Matter is not eternal, the universe has an intelligent Personality in back of it, an Architect, a Builder, and a Sustainer.

Life of Christ, 26

I worship you, O God, for you alone designed and built the universe, and you sustain it.

Foreknowledge and Predestination

To understand the knowledge of God you must make a distinction between foreknowledge and predetermination. The two are not identical. God does foreknow everything, but He does not predetermine us independently of our will and merits.

Your Life Is Worth Living, 16

~

I am awestruck, Lord, to realize that you know all about me before I freely choose to speak or act.

A Mysterious Transformation

Looking into a sunset, the face takes on a golden glow. Looking at the Eucharistic Lord for an hour transforms the heart in a mysterious way as the face of Moses was transformed after his companionship with God on the mountain.

Treasure in Clay, 188–189

I adore you, O Christ, in your Eucharistic presence.

Companionate Care

Only when I am as weak and helpless as my neighbor can I help him. Then there is no spirit of judgment, no sense of superiority, no superciliousness, no looking down one's nose at others. I am his companion in repentance.

Footprints in a Darkened Forest, 100

~

May I always serve the poor, Lord, with spiritual friendship as well as with worldly goods.

Tender and Comprehensive

The foundation of all true sympathy, and that which makes it universal, is love. The best of men can offer only human tenderness without understanding the mystery of pain and tears. But when one comes to the love of Christ, one finds both the tenderness of the human and the comprehensiveness of the Divine.

Footprints in a Darkened Forest, 108

When I find someone in pain, Lord, may I always respond with love and care.

Uncontrolled Desires

Uncontrolled desires grow like weeds and stifle the spirit. Material possessions bring a relative pleasure for a time, but sooner or later a malaise is experienced; a sense of emptiness, a feeling that something is wrong comes over the soul. This is God's way of saying that the soul is hungry and that He alone can satisfy it.

Peace of Soul, 28–29

I am hungry for you, Lord God, and thirsting for your mercy.

A Personal Encounter

Neither theological knowledge nor social action alone is enough to keep us in love with Christ unless both are preceded by a personal encounter with Him.

Treasure in Clay, 190

~

Come, Lord Jesus, and reveal yourself to me.

Christ Chose Death for Us

Though [Christ] came to die, He insisted that it would be voluntary, and not because He would be too weak to defend Himself from His enemies. The only cause for His death would be love, as He told Nicodemus:

> God loved the world so much that he gave his only Son, that everyone who has faith in him may not die but have eternal life. (John 3:16)

Life of Christ, 91

~

Lord Jesus, I thank you for the gift of eternal life that you gave me from the cross.

Strength from Above

Once God entered the created order on the level of humanity and became part of the stream of history, He gave man a new strength from above; He gave him a Divine Power along with human power. In a word, God became man in order that man might become God-like.

The Prodigal World, 4

~

I am grateful, God, that you became a man so that I could become God-like.

Christ Walked Among Us

The galaxy of suns and starry worlds may boast of bulk and size and speed, but we too have our boast: Christ walked *our* earth.

Old Errors and New Labels, 30

~

What a marvel, Lord Jesus, that you who are God
came to earth as a man and dwelt among us!

Christmas Is Happening

Christmas is not something that happened, such as the Battle of Waterloo; it is something that is *happening*. What happened to the human nature, which Christ took from Mary by her consent, can happen in a lesser manner, to our human nature, by our free consent.

The True Meaning of Christmas, 23–26

~

Be present in me, Lord Jesus, and let me make you present in all my encounters.

The Birth of the Mystical Body

Since the Head and the Body are inseparable, it is therefore true to say that as Mary bore Christ in her womb she was virtually carrying the whole Mystical Body. The mother earth that bears the vine also bears the branches.

The Mystical Body of Christ, 318

Mary, I thank you for your yes that made you the Mother of the Church and my Mother.

God Became a Baby

Into this world with its depression, its despair, and its despondency, God came. And He came to set men and their world right with God—not only their hearts and their souls, but even their businesses, their secular affairs, their governments, and their all.... He saved it from its ills by being born as a Babe in the insignificant village of Bethlehem.

The Prodigal World, 3

~

Lord Jesus, I celebrate your birth; you came as a man to set everything right for us.

God Among Beasts

In the filthiest place in the world, a stable, Purity was born. He, Who was later to be slaughtered by men acting as beasts, was born among beasts. He, Who would call Himself the "living Bread descended from heaven," was laid in a manger, literally, a place to eat.

Life of Christ, 27

Lord Jesus, I'm awestruck to realize that you who would feed me with living bread would be laid in a manger, a place to eat.

The Bridge Rebuilt

The bridge between man and God had been broken down; only one who was both God and man could rebuild it. Being man, Christ could act as a man and for man; being God, His Redemption of man would have an infinite value.

Philosophies at War, 61

Thank you, Lord Jesus, for rebuilding the bridge that united me with God.

Looking Down to Heaven

For centuries humans looked up to the heavens and said: "God is way up there." But when the mother held the Child in her arms, it could be truly said that she looked *down* to heaven. Now God was "way down here" in the dust of human lives.

Three to Get Married, 153

~

I celebrate your birth, O Lord, which brought heaven down to earth.

New Creatures

He who from all eternity was born of the Eternal Father was born in time in Bethlehem. He wills that we, who are born in time of our earthly fathers, should be reborn in Eternity of the Heavenly Father, made new creatures, possessed of new life, and members of the Kingdom of God.

The Prodigal World, 7

⁓

I present myself to you, O God, as a new creature, reborn from above and rejoicing in my new life.

Doing the Truth

Truth is not just something to be believed in, but to be acted out. Once we possess it and it possesses us, we become something very different than we were before. The true life therefore is one which responds faithfully to all God's influences and which says in its joy: "My soul waits on the Lord" (Psalm 33:20).

Way to Inner Peace, 157

~

O God, I pledge to be a doer of the word and not just a hearer only.

God's Love

What has revealed the love of God, where we are concerned, is that He has sent His Only Begotten Son into the world so that we might have life through Him. That love resides not in our showing any love for God, but in His showing love for us first. . . .

The True Meaning of Christmas, 8

Your love, O Lord, astounds me, saves me, supports me, and encourages me.

Bibliography

The Writings of Archbishop Fulton J. Sheen

Characters of the Passion. Liguori, MO: Liguori/Triumph,1998.

Children and Parents. New York: Simon and Schuster, 1957.

The Cross and the Beatitudes. Liguori, MO: Liguori/Triumph, 2000.

The Cross and the Crisis. Milwaukee: The Bruce Publishing Company, 1938.

The Divine Romance. New York: Alba House, 1996.

The Eternal Galilean. New York: Alba House, 1997.

Footprints in a Darkened Forest. New York: Meredith Press, 1967.

For God and Country. New York: P.J. Kenedy & Sons, 1941.

Go to Heaven. New York: McGraw-Hill Book Company, Inc., 1960.

God and War. New York: P.J. Kenedy & Sons, 1942.

Guide to Contentment. New York: Alba House, 1996.

The Life of All Living. Garden City, NY: Garden City Books, 1951.

Life of Christ. New York: Doubleday Image, 1977.

Life Is Worth Living. Chicago: Ignatius Press, 1999.

Lift Up Your Heart. Liguori, MO: Liguori/Triumph, 1997.

Light Your Lamps. Huntington, IN: Our Sunday Visitor, 1947.

Love One Another. New York: P.J. Kenedy & Sons, 1944.

Moods and Truths. Garden City, NY: Garden City Books, 1950.

The Mystical Body of Christ. New York: Sheed and Ward, 1935.

Old Errors and New Labels. Garden City, NY: Garden City Books, 1950.

On Being Human. Garden City, NY: Doubleday, 1982.

Peace of Soul. Garden City, NY: Garden City Books, 1951.

Philosophies at War. New York: Charles Scribner's Sons, 1943.

The Power of Love. New York: Image Books, 1968.

Preface to Religion. New York: P.J. Kenedy & Sons, 1946.

The Prodigal World. New York: Alba House, 2003.

The Rainbow of Sorrows. New York: P.J. Kenedy & Sons, 1938.

Religion Without God. Garden City, NY: Garden City Books, 1954.

St. Thérèse: A Treasured Love Story. Irving: TX: Basilica Press, 2007.

The Seven Capital Sins. New York: Alba House, 2005.

The Seven Last Words. Garden City, NY: Garden City Books, 1952.

Seven Pillars of Peace. New York: Charles Scribner's Sons, 1944.

The Seven Virtues. Garden City, NY: Garden City Books, 1953.

Thinking Life Through. New York: McGraw-Hill Book Company, Inc., 1955.

Those Mysterious Priests. New York: Alba House, 2010.

Three to Get Married. New York: Scepter Publishers, 1996.

Treasure in Clay: The Autobiography of Fulton J. Sheen. New York: Doubleday Image, 1982.

The True Meaning of Christmas. Fort Collins, CO: Roman Catholic Books, 1955.

Victory Over Vice. Garden City, NY: Garden City Books, 1953.

Way to Inner Peace. New York: Alba House, 1995.

The World's First Love. San Francisco: Ignatius Press, 1996.

Your Life Is Worth Living. Schnecksville, PA: St. Andrew's Press, 2001.